The Neighborhood
(1935-1955)

(N)

Kirkwood Avenue

Jones

Kirkwood Court

(Playing field)

1126 McCarty

1302 Boice

Lower Muscatine Road

Dunlap Farm

Ginter Avenue

1215 Carney Arnett

1205 Duncan

1215 Diehl

1219 Sage

1223 Albrizio

1202 Greene Sheets

1206 Blome

1210 Brinkhouse miller

1214 Allen Cumiskey January

1218 DeGowin (1)

1213 Risley Rundell

1215 Okerbloom

Cornfield

Pickard Street

1217

1202 Oliver

1218 Engel

1217 Olson

vacant lot

Friendly Avenue

1111 Tompkins Gage mason

1203 DeGowin (2)

1217 Bunge

1301 Butterfield

1302 macy

1305 Gregory megrew Plattner

Yewell Street

Ridge Street

1325 Updegraff

Kaminsky

Williamson

Highland Avenue

Gottleib

Cottonwood Avenue

Davtvemont Anderlik Frantz

FARM HOUSE

House of Moffitt:

The First 20 Years
-A Memoir-

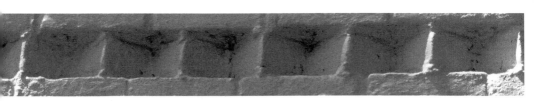

Richard L. DeGowin

Ice Cube Press, LLC (Est. 1993)
North Liberty, Iowa

House of Moffitt: The First 20 Years, A Memoir
Copyright © 2014 Richard L. DeGowin
Foreword © 2014 Nicholas Johnson

Isbn 9781888160833

Library of Congress Control Number: 2014951491

Ice Cube Press, LLC (Est. 1993)
205 N. Front Street
North Liberty, Iowa 52317
www.icecubepress.com
steve@icecubepress.com
twitter: @icecubepress

The paper used in this publication meets the minimum requirements of the American National Standard for Information Sciences—Permanence of Paper for Printed Library Materials, ANSI Z39.48-1992.

Manufactured in the United States of America.

for Karen and Bill

Contents

HOUSE OF MOFFIT, cover photo: The cover shows an image of the house Howard and Anna Moffitt lived in during their last years in Iowa City: 1939-1943. Growing up in Iowa City, both the author and the publisher of this monograph have admired, since childhood, this charming dwelling on Kirkwood Avenue. Iowa City native, John Dyson, admired this house as a young man, never imagining one day it would be his, but when he learned it was for sale, John and wife Maralee, availed themselves of the opportunity to acquire this home where they have resided for 42 years. As Howard Moffitt added a wing to the original small house, John and Maralee made additions to modernize this elegant home on a lovely tree-lined street where Iowa's Civil War Governor, Samuel J. Kirkwood, once lived.

Foreword

This book is, first of all, Dr. Richard L. DeGowin's story. It's not a 700-page "autobiography," as you must have noticed by now if you are holding it. It's rather a collection of vignettes from his life, described with as much detail and color as a white page with black type permits. Indeed, the reader may think he or she is holding the work of a novelist when they read:

> His movements were quick, yet his speech betrayed a rural twang, so one's first impressions of Dr. Moyers in mufti did not permit one to accurately speculate on his career. This short, wiry, clean-shaven man with light brown hair and glasses had grown up in a small town in southwest Iowa. In addition to his work as an ordained Presbyterian Minister, he performed as a trick rider in rodeos. Employed as a carpenter to defray his college and dental school expenses…he had worked summers for Moffitt, helping to build our house… (pg 138)

To save your looking it up, the Islamic word "mufti" comes to us via Britain and refers to "civilian attire," in this instance, I gather, a medical doctor who forgot his white coat.

The author's observations and comments range from descriptive to reflective, humorous to poignant—interweaving the observations of a five-year-old boy with his mother at the 1939 New York World's Fair with an adult's perspective on The Great Depression and World War II. Together, this mosaic provides a rich, coherent picture of the life of this accomplished man, alone worth reading for the insight and joy it provides about him.[1]

But the book's appeal to a variety of audiences goes well beyond that.

As the book's title reveals, one subject and potential audience that may have been among the author's original motivations, reflects his research regarding what he calls the "House of Moffitt." This is not a reference to an American equivalent of a British royal family, such as, perhaps, "The House of Bush," or "The House of Kennedy." Nor is it the inspiring story of a young entrepreneur who started the successful chain of Moffitt's Muffins outlets, as in the "International House of Pancakes."

It is, rather, DeGowin's significant contribution to the history and literature regarding a rather remarkable mid-Twentieth-Century home building effort. The Moffitt houses involved the unique design, materials, building techniques, motives, economics, business acumen, impact on a community, and politics of a man named Howard Moffitt. Moffitt was, among other things, willing to rent homes at reasonable rates in Iowa City, Iowa,—what today we might call "affordable housing." For anyone interested in the history, impact, occupants (including the DeGowin family), and other persons involved with Moffitt houses, this book is destined to become the go-to first source they should consult.[2]

The book is also a contribution to the American history of what we call The Great Depression and World War II—along with the World's Fair

---

1 ["A Tour of the East (21OCT-4 NOV 1939),"Ch. VII, University Elementary School 1939-46; Ch. VI, The Great Depression.
2 Ch. III, Moffitt Houses; ch. IV, Yewell Street Neighbors; Ch. XVIII 1203 Friendly Avenue 1946-1955; Ch. XXIV Friends of Moffitt Houses.

of 1939. The author's contribution is not revealed on the grand canvas used by conventional historians, but rather—to borrow the macro-micro distinction of the economists—at the micro level of their impact on one boy and his family in one American city.

> [W]e grew vegetables in our Victory Garden.... [Mother] saved in tin cans, grease for munitions manufacture, and flattened other empty tin cans, turning them in to scrap metal drives for the war effort.

> My friends and I collected newspapers, old tires, inner tubes and scrap metal for Boy Scouts...scrap drives. We pasted 10-cent savings stamps in a little booklet until...redeem[ing] them for a $25 US War Savings Bond....[O]ur consumer habits of the Great Depression prepared us for austerity during WWII. (pg 126)

The impact of those overwhelming historical events aside, the book is also sprinkled with descriptions of what life was like in general for children growing up in Iowa during the 1930s and 1940s, both life on a farm (a short walk from Dick's house at "99th and Plowed Ground") and in a university town—the freedom they had to roam, the activities they created for themselves, their clubs, and their schools.

> [G]rowing up in our south side Moffitt neighborhood, no one locked the doors of his house or automobile....[I]t was not unusual to find a neighbor standing in our living room, having entered without knocking, announcing herself to my mother with, "Yoo-Hoo, Laura." (pg 55)

> Boys and girls, their dogs yelping at their heels, ran freely all over the neighborhood, playing tag, hide and seek, kick the can, and

king on the hill....Older kids played softball, touch or tackle football, or bicycle polo. Later, there were war games. (pg 55)

Boys cut grass with push reel lawn mowers and weeds with sickles....Fans served to cool bodies, somewhat, by evaporating sweat from perspiring skin in the summer, and without air conditioning...life slowed down, and school didn't start until after Labor Day. (pg. 63)

Many days after school...found me walking east on Ginter Avenue's dirt extension from Yewell Street to the Dunlap farm to play with Jimmy [in] the haymow of his barn....Swinging from ropes hanging from rafters.... (pg. 128)

His early jobs did not end with push reel lawn mowers. Among other things before he became Dr. DeGowin, Dick delivered newspapers to the neighbors, served food at the University of Iowa Hospital Employees' Cafeteria, serviced automobiles, was part of a county surveying crew, and worked "in" cement for a contractor.[3]

The reference above to "their schools" meant, for Dick DeGowin, something special that no longer exists—an elementary and high school run, not by a local school board, but by a college of education: the University Elementary and High School of the University of Iowa's College of Education. (As Dick puts it, "my teachers showed me how to acquire, retain, analyze, and use information for work and pleasure, and how to communicate verbally and in writing." (pg 143)

---

3 Ch. XIX, Summer Jobs.

Those interested in educational research and innovation, indeed in K-12 education generally, will find the memories and reflections about this part of Dick's life of special interest.[4]

As the son of an internationally known and honored medical doctor and professor, Dick ultimately decided on a medical career of his own. His tales of the challenges of medical school will certainly be of interest to those who have undergone such experiences themselves, those who are now in medical school, and any readers who are curious as to what their own doctor may have experienced. (Dick's father, Dr. Elmer DeGowin, discovered the procedures for the preservation of blood, and established "the longest continuously operating [blood bank] in the United States"— the one in the University of Iowa Hospital in Iowa City that bears his name today.[5]

There are probably better sources than this book for the thorough study of the vocabulary of medicine. But just as any working person will tend to notice in others that which they know best—such as their car, hairstyle, or designer clothes—the reader will find sprinkled throughout the book, intermixed with the results of Dr. DeGowin's gift of detailed observation and description of people, whatever may have struck him about the person's medical condition, diseases, and prescriptions in the language he might have used with a fellow physician. It's an insight into how our doctor friends may view us as well; but not to worry, the medical jargon is rare, and usually more amusing than distracting. He didn't just have some "medical problems at birth."

---

4 See generally, Ch. VII, University Elementary School 1939-1946; Ch. XIV, University High School 1946-1952; Ch. XVII, 50th Reunion of U-High Class of 1952.

5 "The Blood Bank," Ch. IX, Banking Blood.

[At birth Dick] greeted the light of day with several disturbing features, neonatal jaundice and a large cephalohematoma [followed shortly after by] staphylococcal dermatitis... .(pg. 33)

I have a "back pain." Dick's father, by contrast, had "inflammation of paraspinal ligaments . . .." (pg. 131) One man "was recognized for his discovery of primary aldosteronism . . .." (pg. 206) He describes another person as having "a generous paunch from a love of food and a history of hypothyroidism." (pg. 207)

Here's what Dick was doing in class while others at Michigan were drinking beer:

I worked [helping a] laboratory technician grow Ehrlich Ascites Tumor Cells in the peritoneal cavities of mice. We harvested the cells...and injected them into rabbits to make antisera. Later, we obtained plasma from the rabbits and titered their antisera. Then we injected the antisera into mice . . ..(pg. 203)

And Dick's dog? You guessed it:

Shorty was a lovable black and white mongrel dog, who in his former life served with distinction as a talented experimental subject at The University of Chicago. He had learned to lie quietly and breathe through the tube of an apparatus that measured his basal metabolic rate, [then] a useful...test of thyroid function.(pg. 35)

The reader will also occasionally come upon candid revelations of the author's political and ideological positions—first developed by him at a very early age. ("[A]s an eight-year-old child, I voiced my fears...that Franklin Roosevelt...might become a dictator like the enemy's axis leaders

. . .." "A good democratic government rules by the will of a free people whose elected leaders trust their constituents to freely possess and use guns . . .."(pg, 124) He writes that, "the blame laid on George Bush for the Great Recession…resulted from policies initiated in the Carter Administration…and expanded by the Clinton Administration…." (pg. 61) If Dick's views square with those of the reader, he or she will be warmed and reassured to find themselves with agreeable company in these pages. If not, it's worthwhile to reflect upon what the author says, thereby gaining insight into a well-educated man's thinking that is shared by a very large proportion of the American body politic today.

On a personal note, aside from politics, Dick and I have lived lives on closely parallel tracks. (Even as to politics, it is my memory—not in this book—that with his mother's instruction on political process, he and I went door-to-door together, circulating a petition that played a role in the ultimate location of a swimming pool in the Iowa City Park.) We are within four months of each other in age, both born in the mid-1930s, to college educated parents whose marriages held for a lifetime ("privileged to grow up in families where…mothers and fathers stayed together…." (pg. 20). We both grew up in small families, in the same university-dominated community, an Iowa county seat town surrounded by farmland, with fathers who were university professors. We went through 13 years of school together, and shared many of the same activities—including band,[6] debate,[7] and what Dick calls "The Johnson County Bureau of Investigation."[8]

---

6 Ch. XVI, The Music Man.

7 "The Debate," Ch. XIV, University High School 1946-1952.

8 Ch. XV, The Johnson County Bureau of Investigation

This was followed by college and our graduate educations (his in medicine, mine in law). We both had wives named Karen (mine deceased, his still living), families, and careers. Both my Karen, and my wife of 25 years, Mary Vasey, were also members of the U-High Colossal Class of 1952—a statistically significant percentage of all the women in our class, and a tribute to their quality (as well as their tolerance of their less-accomplished male classmates). Indeed, I even figure from time to time in these pages.

Thus, my fascination with Dick's book comes, in many ways, from the fact it is my story as well as his. I have nothing like the power of memory that he displays in these pages. As a result, if I ever do undertake a comparable bit of writing, much of it—with credit to him of course—will probably draw upon what he has recalled. If you are near our ages, and share any of our prior locations, schools, professions or activities, you may find this book additionally appealing for that reason as well.

Nicholas Johnson
www.nicholasjohnson.org
Iowa City, Iowa
August, 2014

Preface

A few years ago, twelve fellow students in Jim McKean's week-long course, Memoirs, in the Iowa Summer Writing Festival, expressed interest and critiqued an excerpt about Moffitt Houses, a part of a narrative of our family history I had written for my son, Bill. Returning to Iowa City after an absence of 16 years had led me to reflect that my experience growing up in Iowa City was quite different from Bill's. The first 20 years of his life there, from 1970 to 1990, encompassed a relatively stable period, whereas my first 20 years living in Iowa City from 1935 to 1955 began during the Great Depression and lasted through World War II, the Korean War, and the Cold War, with its threat of annihilation in an atomic holocaust.

While writing this narrative, I became seriously ill. I survived, thanks to the skilled care of my colleagues, physicians, and nurses, in The University of Iowa Cancer Center and in The University of Iowa Hospitals and Clinics. Grateful for the reprieve, I grasped a chance to record for Bill and other readers, my recollections of living in Howard Moffitt's affordable housing and my impressions of events that occurred during that time. My memory is imperfect, and my comments reflect a point of view derived from a fondness of reading American history. Although many of the opinions that I have expressed are probably not politically correct, they are not intended to offend.

If one alleged that I was privileged to live at a special time in a special place, I would have to agree. However, not one of my friends, nor did I come from a family of great wealth, nor did we become wealthy ourselves, but we were privileged to grow up in families where our mothers and fathers stayed together even though they shouted at each other when they disagreed, like mine did. Our parents worked hard to feed, clothe, and shelter us without government assistance, disciplining us to respect others and encouraging our aspirations for formal education, supporting some of us through graduate school.

With this narrative, I hope to express my admiration for my parents, my classmates, my teachers, and for Howard Moffitt and other residents of Iowa City who took advantage of the opportunities afforded them living in a small Midwestern college town in the "flyover zone."

Richard L. DeGowin
Iowa City, Iowa
October, 2014

Introduction

This is a story about the author's experience growing up in America's Heartland during the Great Depression, World War II, and the Cold War—cataclysmic events of the 20th Century. I lived in affordable housing provided by Howard Moffitt who rented out more than 100 houses in Iowa City, Iowa. As a child I remember seeing our landlord, Howard Moffitt, a tall slender active man with a thin mustache, sporting a suit and tie, when he appeared in our Yewell Street neighborhood at the behest of one of his renters.

Articles I discovered in the Winter 1992 issue of the *Palimpsest* impressed me with Moffitt's entrepreneurial spirit, his ability to see and capitalize on opportunities available to Americans, even in the midst of dire economic times. I am indebted to those authors who have given us biographical data of Howard Moffitt and information about his work by recording interviews of his family members, friends, coworkers, and others in the *Palimpsest* 73:147-160, 1992: Phil Miller: "Howard Moffitt's Small Homes and Small Cottages," pp. 147-156; Jan Nash: "The Shift to Small Homes," pp. 156-158; Jeff Schabilion: "Living in a Moffitt House," pp. 159-160; and Linda Brown-Link: "Affordable Housing and True Artistry," p. 160. An application for the National Register of Historic Places, prepared in 1992 by Jan Nash: *The Small Homes of Howard F. Moffitt in Iowa City and Coralville, Iowa 1924-1943*, is a treasure of information about Moffitt houses and their significance.

From these enjoyable well-written pieces, we learn that Howard Francis Moffitt was born in 1893 in Afton, Iowa, moving with his family in 1911 to Oxford, Iowa, a small town near Iowa City, Iowa, and graduating from high school with classmate Hugh Dunlap two years later. After earning a bachelor's degree in political science at The University of Iowa, Moffitt and Dunlap trained as pilots in the Army Air Corps, but World War I ended before they deployed to Europe. Moffitt then traveled in the West, attended law school for a while and worked in stores in Waterloo and Iowa City, Iowa.

Forming a partnership in Iowa City with Ray Blakesley, their Triangle Auto Supply boasted eight stores in southeast Iowa by 1927. Without experience in home construction, in 1924 the pair built their first house on Rundell Street, accommodated by a trolley that ran on tracks down the middle of the street to convey neighborhood residents down town. Moffitt saw the need for affordable rental housing in this university community where graduate students and struggling young instructors might live for a few years to complete their degrees or move on to tenure-track positions in academe. His former classmate, Hugh Dunlap, and the other principal contractors during the 1920's and 1930's built houses for sale, not for rent. Iowa City was, and is now, a very active real estate market. For 20 years, from 1924 to the 1940's, Moffitt and Blakesley built over 100 small homes to rent and may have owned over 200, each different in configuration and appearance—no cookie-cutter homogeneity—but identifiable by massive stone, brick or stucco chimneys, stone veneer siding, soaring roof lines, and integrated one-car garages.

A friend and resident of Iowa City for over 40 years, Bill Nowysz, who as an architect designed more than 50 homes in town, was asked to help remodel many Moffitt homes for their owners. He told me that Moffitt used good quality building materials, recycled from their former employment and incorporated into his houses with good quality workmanship—"no shoddy workmanship." Wood tongue-in-groove paneling lining de-accessioned railroad boxcars found many uses in construction of doors, walls, and roofs. Railroad ties served as lintels for doors and windows, while rails from the later defunct Rundell Street Trolley supported floor joists.

Brick, salvaged from demolished buildings, went for siding. Rubble limestone scraps from nearby quarries and salvage stone foundation blocks served as veneer siding, the mortar skillfully indented to show off the edges of shaped stones laid in linear patterns, giving a pleasing appearance. Moffitt's masons sometimes applied a decorative saw-tooth pattern of brick as lintels above some doors and windows. Interiors were cozy, intimate and interestingly person-friendly, but did not accommodate large furniture.

Designs of the homes came from various sources; magazine articles in *House Beautiful, American Home,* from consultations with Moffitt's wife, Anna Glasgow Moffitt, and from Eleanor Hageboeck, a renter with a background in Art History who worked on floor plans and interior design. From an interview with Hugh Dunlap on 28JUL1992, Jan Nash recorded: "Moffitt once asked Iowa City builder Hugh Dunlap, who had been academically trained, to design some house plans for him. However, when presented with the plans, Moffitt decided they were too expensive and never accepted them."

Jan Nash suggests in her *Palimpsest* article that the Small House Services Bureau of the United States (part of the American Institute of Architects) and Herbert Hoover's Better Homes Movement "brought a sort of national endorsement of small Period houses." "Moffitt's houses," Jan Nash wrote, "fell principally into what is known as Period houses, popular styles of the day which referenced European medieval architecture, as well as early Spanish and East Coast Colonial influences from this country." A brick Moffitt house on 7th Avenue showed a Flemish influence, according to Phil Miller.

In addition to appreciating the need for affordable housing, and finding supplies of recycled but good quality building materials, Moffitt benefited during the Great Depression from an abundance of inexpensive skilled and unskilled labor. This was augmented each summer by high school and college students needing jobs in this university town of 12,000 to 15,000 people.

Moffitt built houses in areas where he could purchase land cheaply, planting neighborhoods in the former flood plain of Ralston Creek and on the periphery of Iowa City, bordering farm land: he colonized Rundell Street, Muscatine Avenue, 7th Avenue, Yewell Street, Cottonwood, Friendly Avenue, Pickard, and Ginter with clusters of his houses, adding single houses in isolated lots on Grant, Dearborn, Jackson, Sheridan, Fairview, College, and Highland, still standing in good shape and occupied for more than 80 years. I have never heard that a Moffitt house was torn down to be replaced.

Price controls imposed by the Roosevelt Administration during World War II froze Moffitt's monthly rents of $30-$50 for his small homes. When his request to raise his rents to $55 per month was refused, my father and other grateful renters wrote to government officials in Washington, D.C. requesting that they exempt our landlord from the regulation so that he would be permitted to raise their rents. Can you imagine that?!

Whether it was frustration with persistent rigid rent controls, or his restless entrepreneurial spirit—manifest by numerous ventures to stay solvent including developing an indoor miniature golf course in the Iowa City Triangle Auto Supply Store, a dealership of McCormick-Deering farm equipment and sales of lump coal for home heating—Howard and Anna Moffitt sold on contract to their renters at $55 per month (6% interest) most of his houses in Iowa City during and after World War II and moved to McAllen, Texas, in 1943. If you think about it, the story of Moffitt's 20 years as a small businessman landlord shows how big government bureaucracy stifled an entrepreneur's efforts to provide affordable housing at no cost to the taxpayer.

In Texas, Moffitt and a partner developed orchards of orange and grape-fruit trees and planned the town of Citrus, Texas, all of which failed to reach fruition. But Moffitt outlived many of his renters, dying in McAllen on 25NOV1982, having survived almost 90 years.

After returning to Iowa City from living in Chicago for 13 years, the title of a novel by Thomas Wolfe, *You Can't Go Home Again*, kept running through my thoughts. The town of my nativity had changed since my first 20 years living in a Moffitt house there. In his book, *People in Quandries*, Wendell Johnson began Chapter II, page 23: "Heraclitus the Greek cast a long shadow before him. He contended that one cannot step in the same river twice." On page 24 the author wrote, "Change is terrifying only to those who, in planning their lives, leave it out of account." I leave it to the reader to decide what has changed for the better and what has changed for the worse.

Chapter I
A New Deal 1932-1935

It was in the depth of the Great Depression, when my father-to-be arrived on the train from Chicago to Iowa City, Iowa. On that hot summer day the First of July 1932, after joining the University of Iowa as Instructor of Internal Medicine, he shared with his new faculty colleagues a 5% cut in salary. At least now he had a job after losing his on the faculty of the University of Michigan in June.

He and his two colleagues had one year to go on their three-year contracts specifying salary raises for each at $200 per year, inducing administrative bean counters at Michigan to gleefully conclude something like, "Hey, if we fire these three instructors now, we could save $600 this year and hire replacements at lesser salaries."

Breaking the contracts of my father and his colleague Dr. Roger O. Egeberg lost Michigan two physicians who attained national recognition, my father as a pioneer in the field of the storage and transfusion of whole blood, and Roger Egeberg who became General MacArthur's doctor and his Aide-de-Camp during World War II, accompanying the General—captured in the iconic Carl Mydans photo on the cover of *Life Magazine*—wading ashore at Luzon, the Philippines on 9 January 1945, keeping MacArthur's famous promise, "I shall return." Later, Dr. Egeberg became in succession: Dean of The University of Southern California School of Medicine, Assistant Secretary for Health and Scientific Affairs of the Department of Health Education and Welfare, and finally, Special Consultant to the President of the United States on Health Affairs from 1971-1979.

As secretary and technician for Dr. Frank N. Wilson, eminent cardiologist and inventor of unipolar electrocardiography, my mother held on to her good job in the Heart Station of the University of Michigan until her husband decided whether he would stay at Iowa. Meanwhile, my dad shared a room in the Quadrangle Dormitory that summer with Dr. Reuben Flocks, another new instructor just arrived from Johns Hopkins Medical School, from which a letter of recommendation written in 1932 by his former Hopkins department head, discovered in a Urology Department file at Iowa 80 years later, reportedly praised Dr. Flocks's abilities and potential yet said, "but he is not really one of us."

Dr. Flocks achieved international recognition as Professor and Head, Department of Urology at Iowa and for his innovative brachytherapy with radioactive gold to treat prostate cancer—Hopkins loss, Iowa's gain. So in July 1932, Dr. Flocks and my dad became life-long friends, caring for patients for over 40 years in The University of Iowa Hospitals where, in their last days, their colleagues cared for them as patients.

THE UNIVERSITY OF IOWA HOSPITALS & CLINICS
While Howard Moffitt started building houses on the east side of Iowa City in the 1920's, the Legislature of the State of Iowa faced making a decision that should have been easy; i.e., how to come up with $2,250,000 to match a grant from the Rockefeller Foundation to build a new University Hospital and Medical Laboratories Building for $4.5 million on the west side of the Iowa River. Well, they did, and after laying its cornerstone

in 1928, they saw it become, with over 1000 beds, the largest university-owned teaching hospital in the country. Approaching Iowa City on Highway 6 from the west, patients saw from miles distant the hospital's Gothic tower, crowning an impressive brick eight-story symmetrical structure sited on a hill.

With passage of the Perkins Act in 1915 and the Haskell-Klaus Act of 1919, the people of Iowa, through the actions of their State Representatives, cast a safety net for the health care of their indigent neighbors. Transported from their homes in the hospital's ambulance service so that they could receive care at the University Hospital, the poor found that their hospital bills were paid by their county, and no physician fees were submitted. Mr. Robert E. Neff and his secretary administered the nursing, pharmacy, dietary, housekeeping, and maintenance staffs of this huge complex.

So it was in this brand new hospital that my father started his seven-day work week as physician attending on one of the four 32-bed Internal Medicine wards, caring for private patients in his office (all fees went to the departmental chairman), attending on the small private service, developing the Allergy Clinic, teaching medical students, interns and residents, and performing research in his lab at night and on weekends.

As a kid, I well remember accompanying Dad to the hospital on Sundays, seeing the terrazzo floors, the institutional green walls and high concrete ceiling beams, now hidden by an extreme makeover of the old hospital. No more will you see, as I did, the outside walls of the clinics lined by bare, shiny brown wood benches and arm chairs, polished by scores of patients waiting for their appointments, cooled in the summer by oscillating fans; no air conditioning.

During the "revolution" of 1946, the physicians in the College of Medicine converted to full-time faculty members with fees from the care of private patients deposited in departmental accounts and salaries set by the Dean, leading to an exodus of Department Heads—unwilling to cope with academic incomes—to enter private practice: Peterson of Surgery, Alcock of Urology, Steindler of Orthopedics, and Obrien of Ophthalmology. My father's salary then, 18 years after graduating from medical school, was $300 per month, the same starting salary my wife, Karen, earned as an Orthoptic Technician working in the Eye Department at The University of Chicago, the only other medical school in the country with a full-time salaried faculty in the 1940's.

THE FAMILY REUNITED

In that same historic year of 1932—it was the same year my father arrived in Iowa—Herbert Hoover, born in West Branch, Iowa, 10 miles east of Iowa City, nominated in June at the Republican Convention, was running for reelection as President of the United States. A self-made man, orphaned at age eleven, a millionaire at age 40, a humanitarian called to feed the starving children during World War I, introducing programs like the Reconstruction Finance Program to ameliorate the misery of the Great Depression, faced an impossible challenge. Anyone, blamed as he was for an economic disaster he predicted, tried to prevent, and had no control over, could never be reelected.

In his book, *The Life of Herbert Hoover: Fighting Quaker 1928-1933*, the author Glen Jeansomme, asked the reader if Hoover was booed for not fixing the Great Depression in 3 years, why was Roosevelt cheered for not fixing it in 6 years? He wrote, "In 1939, the unemployment rate after six years of the New Deal was 17.2% as opposed to 15.9% in 1931."

Despite warnings from her urbane Ann Arbor friends that she could expect frequent encounters with Native Americans if she settled in Iowa on the edge of civilization, my mother joined my dad in Iowa City in February 1933, and nearly froze walking downtown from their rented house on Muscatine Avenue to get supper when their car wouldn't start.

In fact, the end of the Black Hawk War, 100 years earlier (2AUG1832), opened Iowa to settlement by whites. Black Hawk, a Sauk war chief, died as a parolee to Chief Keokuk in southeast Iowa in 1838, the year Iowa became a US Territory. Most members of the Sauk and Fox (Meskwaki) tribes had removed to Kansas in 1847, the year after Iowa was granted statehood with its capital in Iowa City, but by 1859 nearly all of the Fox had returned to a settlement, not a reservation, on land that they had purchased in Tama County, Iowa. Their population according to the 1930 census, ranged at about several hundred persons, while Ottawa Indians living in "civilized" Michigan that year numbered 1,469.

1934

Fifteen months after my mother's arrival in Iowa City, after ten years of marriage, after Father's 12 years of education following high school, with uncertain employment in the Great Depression, Laura and Elmer DeGowin welcomed me to their family. My father, a physician aware of the increasing risk of age for a mother having a baby with Down's syndrome was relieved that his bride, age 33, had delivered her first child, a normal son.

Well, he wasn't quite normal, because he greeted the light of day with several disturbing features: neonatal jaundice and a large cephalohematoma (bleeding under the scalp secondary to trauma from the application of forceps to facilitate birth). Shortly after birth, impetigo (staphylococcal dermatitis), treated in those days before antibiotics by painting the affected skin with gentian violet, added purple luster, if not regal splendor, to the yellow of his jaundice and the blue of his hematoma. Mother told me in jest that she had considered "throwing the baby out with the bath water."

As a humorous birthday gift, my father secured the hospital chart describing my birth from the Department of Obstetrics at the University of Iowa Hospitals, copied the report before it was destroyed and mailed the copy to me while I was in medical school at the University of Chicago. Everett D. Plass, M.D., Professor and Head of the Department of Obstetrics, affirmed in his hand written notes on 14 May 1934 that after an occiput posterior presentation and hard labor on Laura's part, he had presented her with a 7 lb. 14 oz., 21-inch long male baby. A weak initial cry was followed by a loud protest after a second slap on the buttocks. It was not to be his last. Whereas my father was born during the presidential administration of Theodore Roosevelt, I was born at the beginning of the unprecedented 4-term, 12 year reign of his cousin, Franklin Delano Roosevelt and his wife and cousin, Eleanor Roosevelt.

"By all accounts, 1934 was a remarkable year: Flash Gordon made his first appearance in the comic strips, and Frank Capra's *It Happened One Night*, starring Clark Gable and Claudette Colbert, would go on to win every major Academy Award. In May, one of the worst storms of the Dust Bowl swept away massive heaps of Great Plains topsoil; in August, Adolf Hitler became Germany's new Fuhrer. Pretty Boy Floyd, Baby Face Nelson, Bonnie and Clyde, and John Dillinger were all gunned down in spectacular, tabloid-titillating fashion. On Broadway, Ethel Merman opened in Cole Porter's big new hit, *Anything Goes*; while farther uptown, in Harlem, seventeen-year-old Ella Fitzgerald made her singing debut at the recently christened Apollo Theater;" (Mauro, James: *Twilight at the World of Tomorrow, Genius, Madness, Murder and the 1939 World's Fair on the Brink of War*, Ballantine Books, New York, Chapter 1, p.3, pp. 401, 2010.)

1312 MUSCATINE AVENUE

I remember nothing about my first year of life, but my mother told me that I returned from the hospital to live with her and my father in a bungalow at 1312 Muscatine Avenue in Iowa City, recently rented from a widow whose name I forgot. I shared that humble abode with Shorty, my surrogate until my arrival. Shorty was a lovable black and white mongrel dog, who in his former life served with distinction as a talented experimental subject at The University of Chicago. He had learned to lie quietly and breathe through the tube of an apparatus that measured his basal metabolic rate (BMR), a useful, but now obsolete, test of thyroid function.

It has occurred to me that Shorty's contributions in helping to establish parameters of the BMR may have proved critical in diagnosing Mother's hypothyroidism that followed her recovery from sub-acute thyroiditis. Also, my father relied upon test results obtained with the BMR to recommend treatment for patients in the multidisciplinary Thyroid Clinic, which he established in the 1950's at The University of Iowa Hospitals. Perhaps, unknowingly, I posed a challenge as a sibling rival to Shorty who wandered from home one day and never returned.

The decision to find a new home for our family came shortly after my mother rescued me from becoming flattened fauna. With a newly acquired ability to walk, I had toddled out to explore the street in front of our house, which happened to carry the busy automobile and truck traffic from New York to California as US Highway 6, the predecessor of Interstate 80. I wonder if Shorty had survived the fate from which I was saved.

I regret not asking my parents, or forgetting the answer if I had asked them, how they came to pick our next home, a house rented from Howard F. Moffitt on Yewell Street where we lived for the next eleven years. Had my dad learned about the Moffitt enclave on Yewell Street from his colleague in the small Department of Internal Medicine, Dr. James Greene, who lived in the Moffitt house at 1202 Yewell Street?

Chapter II
1218 Yewell Street 1935-1946

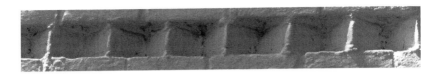

Named after George Yewell, an artist who painted the hills and trees of the Iowa River Valley before the incorporation of Iowa City in 1839, Yewell Street bordered the southeast edge of town. It was paved for three blocks running south from Ginter Avenue until it reached Highland Avenue where, shedding pavement, it turned into gravel and dirt for another block to Cottonwood Avenue, finally terminating in a farmer's lane. Friendly Avenue arose from a small hollow in the west to intersect Yewell after its first block south. After crossing Yewell heading east, Friendly turned into dirt for about 150 feet before ending in Mr. Reagan's cornfield.

When we moved into our white clapboard Moffitt house at 1218 Yewell Street in 1935, it was the last one on the east side the street's first block going south. Four lovely mature American Elms—lost to Dutch Elm disease in the 1960's—shaded our front lawn, and others shaded the front lawns of all of our neighbors. Our lawn stretched across the vacant lot next door to the south where a newer house now stands. No concrete sidewalks usurped the lawn's Kentucky Blue Grass, clover, and weeds my father mowed with an old iron reel-type push lawnmower once a week.

Our backyard extended east about 75 feet to the edge of Mr. Reagan's immense cornfield and contained but one structure, an eco-friendly, solar and wind-powered "clothes dryer" provided by our thoughtful landlord. It consisted of four wire clotheslines strung between the tops of two rusty rectangular chassis frames salvaged from junked Model-T Fords. The opposite ends of the frames were buried in the ground. Children's campsites, fortifications, and a Victory Garden occupied, at various times, the back of the vacant lot next door. A house at 1226 Yewell Street occupies that once vacant lot today.

If you walked up concrete steps and entered our front door, the first thing you encountered was my mother's secondhand upright piano against the north white plaster wall of our living room. On the east wall before coming to the archway to the dining room, stood our wooden floor-model Sears Silvertone AM Radio. Windows with lace curtains flanked a fireplace on the south wall. The one on the east side admitted enough natural light for my father to read as he sat in his big chair and puffed on one of his 8 or 10 pipes selected from a rack on a side table. The table also supported a large white can of Schermerhorn's Pipe Mixture tobacco, a large round ashtray with a centrally placed cork for knocking out ashes, and his old Boy Scout knife for scraping the bowl of his pipe. The large stack of *The Journal of the American Medical Association* never seemed to diminish in height despite my dad's assiduous reading.

A large mahogany veneer dining table, lighted by high windows on the south and east, occupied most of the dining room. Beneath the south window, supported by struts attached to the outside of the house, a long green wooden flower box served as a planter in which my mother nurtured petunias. The window above the white kitchen sink gave Mother a view of our backyard and Mr. Reagan's cornfield to the east. I remember feeling the hot moist wind as it wafted over the fields, rustling leaves of corn on late summer days with temperatures exceeding 100 degrees. Natives said that you could hear the corn grow. The icebox—later replaced by an electric refrigerator—and a white porcelain-finished gas range and stove were opposite the sink. An electric toaster stood on the counter, but there was no electric coffee maker, can opener, or dishwasher.

Our small family of three ate all of our meals together at the dining room table. Mother served our modest supper at 6:00 PM, sharp. One economic dish my father liked was canned baked beans with canned Boston Brown Bread, a molasses-based favorite of his.

My least favorite dish was canned peas boiled in milk, which curdled as I stared at it, nauseated and unwilling to eat it, finally relenting after being told, "You cannot leave the table until you finish your meal. The children in Europe are starving, and we cannot throw away good food."

At the north end of the kitchen, a door opened to basement steps. Our unfinished basement was the coolest place in the house during those dust bowl days of the 1930's, featuring day after day of humidity at 90% and high temperatures in the 100's. Two months after I was born, a high temperature of 118° degrees F. was recorded in Keokuk, Iowa, (20JUL1934). Uncle Ralph, visiting from New Haven in 1935, spent hours with me in the relative cool of the basement, he in shorts, I in diapers—a story he liked to relate many times when I was an adult.

If I entered our front door and turned left, I climbed an enclosed stairway lighted by an arched opening halfway upstairs that looked out over the piano to the living room. Invariably, strains of Tchaikovsky's *The Sleeping Beauty Ballet Suite*, the theme song of the 400 Hour sponsored by the Northwestern Railway on WMAQ Chicago, woke me at 6:00 AM every morning. I remember sitting on the stairs at that arched opening listening to classical music and the sonorous voice of announcer Norman Ross broadcast over our radio as Father sat in his chair reading the *Des Moines*

Register. Without exception, he arose early every day, made breakfast and read the paper before leaving for work at the hospital.

Beyond the unused third bedroom at the head of the stairs, a hall led south, off which was our only bathroom, my parents' bedroom and my bedroom at the end of the hall. My east window looked out over the cornfield to Lower Muscatine and to the tracks of the Rock Island Railroad. I could see a mile distant where the sleek streamlined engines of the Rock Island Rockets pulled shiny silver passenger coaches west to Des Moines, Denver, San Francisco, or east to Chicago. Little did I realize then that in 1952, the Rocket would carry me to Chicago to catch the Michigan Central, arriving in Ann Arbor as a freshman at the University of Michigan. Five years later it would carry my bride, Karen, and me to Chicago for our honeymoon, before I returned to medical school.

Chapter III
Moffitt Houses

From 1935 to 1946, my parents rented our furnished three-bedroom house at 1218 Yewell Street from Howard Moffitt. Rent was $32.50 per month. Our neighbors in this bucolic setting were families of other junior members of the university faculty who considered themselves fortunate to have jobs and live in Mr. Moffitt's affordable housing during the Depression. Although my mother thought Moffitt had not built our house, he had put up many of the 100 or so houses he owned in Iowa City. More than a dozen of his rental homes graced our street and adjacent neighborhoods.

Someone suggested that the small stone-sided houses he built around 1938 on the east side of Muscatine Avenue near its intersection with Court Street resembled cottages in the English Cotswolds. In 1995, they were designated an Iowa City Historic District. Neighborhoods with clusters of his homes like ours bore no resemblance to the post-World War II uniformity of Levittown, New York, because none of his houses looked like another. Their roof lines soared, were steeply pitched, siding was clapboard or stone, and some had inside walls that undulated, failing to meet at precisely right angles. Windows of some were slanted to accommodate salvaged sashes. Some floors sloped to inspire one homeowner to declare that when she placed her child's marble on one side of her kitchen floor, it rolled briskly to the other side without encouragement.

In Moffitt's own whitewashed stone house on the southwest corner of Kirkwood Avenue and Marcy Street, 837 Kirkwood Avenue, the genesis of these unique structures hatched. As the story goes, Mrs. Anna Moffitt, seated comfortably in her living room would pass the open copy of *Better Homes & Gardens* she was reading and remark, "Howard, the house in this picture would look nice in that vacant lot on Ginter Avenue." Tearing out the page featuring the artist's concept of an ivy-covered cottage with its abbreviated floor plan, Howard dutifully folded and pocketed it.

Early next morning, Howard forwarded the torn page with Anna's recommendation to his foreman, Jesse Baker. Jesse, who looked at least 75 years-old—all adults look "old" to a child—wore a hearing aid, a denim shirt partly covered by bib overalls and sported a sweat-stained locomotive engineer's cap made from a mattress ticking fabric. A small paper tag, labeled Red Man Chewing Tobacco, dangled from strings that disappeared into a breast pocket of his Oshkosh-B-Gosh overalls. Brown spittle dribbled from a corner of his mouth to make its way through two days' stubble on his chin, affirming his use of the foul-smelling weed.

Pocketing the "blue prints" he had received, Jesse and his crew drove their flatbed truck to a farm where, with the owner's permission, they tore down an old barn for its lumber. They added their salvage to newer more expensive construction materials purchased from the lumberyard and hauled it all to the new home site.

CONSTRUCTION

Moffitt's recycling of building materials was not an isolated event. Dotty Carney lived across the street, 1215 Pickard Street, from a house Moffitt's men were building at 1203 Friendly Avenue in 1941. She swore to my mother that she had seen the carpenters incorporate into that house under construction, the painted green side boards of Mother's old window flower box, which Jesse had replaced when the bottom rotted out. After the war, my parents bought that house on Friendly Avenue, a block away from our house on Yewell Street. Try as I might, I never located parts of that window box, transferred like DNA from our old house to our new one.

Standing nearby the building site, I learned with great fascination the rudiments of house construction watching Jesse Baker, a creative genius, and his men work. Extracting the crumpled "blueprints" from his pocket, Jesse ordered his men to begin excavating the basement at the site on Ginter Avenue. With white string tied to rusty iron stakes as a guide, 5 young workers began digging with ditching spades. After they had penetrated a foot of sod and black Iowa topsoil with their spades and mattocks, Jesse called in the heavy-duty earth moving equipment; a shiny steel scoop-shovel pulled by a horse and guided by a man grasping two long wooden handles bolted to each side of the scoop. This rig resembling a huge flat-bottom feed scoop, picked up loose dirt and shaved off layers of yellow-brown clay as the "power plant" responded to commands of, "Giddyup! Gee! Haw! Whoa!" With fatigue, entreaties with carrots and sugar cubes were required to activate the horsepower. This excavating equipment lacked the efficiency of a modern diesel bulldozer, but it was a lot quieter and left a smaller carbon footprint.

Studs atop poured concrete basement walls proved diverse in age and origin. Some old fellows seasoned with cow manure had, in their former life, supported the walls of a barn, whereas newer recruits from the lumberyard, green and slightly bowed, retained fragments of bark clinging to their rough sides. Carpenters nailed lath for plaster to the inside of the two-by-four studs, attached boards to the outside, which they covered with tarpaper before applying clapboard siding. Later, they dumped sawdust between the studs, used as Moffitt had observed, as effective insulation in ice houses. Jesse set the pitch of the roof, directing his men handling the beams and trusses, with hand signals and expletives from his vantage point across the street.

Moffitt's renters joked about their homes built with recycled materials, curving walls and sloping floors, but loved Mr. Moffitt, because he was responsive and cared for them. One bright spring morning they saw him walking down the middle of Yewell Street, dressed in his suit and tie for Easter Services, with a replacement toilet seat over his shoulder, responding to a renter's call for help. Speaking of toilet seats, one day my friend Bill Nowysz, the architect, responded to a call from a contractor remodeling a house, who said, "You've got to see this to believe it!" Shortly thereafter, Bill stood amazed looking at a wall the contractor had denuded of plaster to reveal oak toilet seat lids that Moffitt had employed, instead of lath, to hold the plaster wall covering.

During and after World War II, Howard Moffitt sold most of his houses to his renters and moved with Mrs. Moffitt to Texas. A few years later, he returned to Iowa City to visit my father as a patient with a few minor complaints. His entrepreneurial spirit had led him to diversify after divesting his Iowa City real estate holdings of 20 years and purchase orange groves in Texas and a fishing fleet off the coast of New England.

Chapter IV
Yewell Street Neighbors

In the course of thinking about our neighborhood as it was before World War II, I awoke at 5:00 AM one morning, unable to sleep until I had written down the names and vocations of our neighbors who had lived in these rented Moffitt houses. Later, my son Bill, patient with his father's obsession, drove me up and down Yewell Street, permitting me to record my former neighbor's street numbers. It struck me that I had grown up at the edge of an Iowa cornfield with a remarkable group of persons who later achieved positions of leadership in academia. Some, like my father, gained international reputations as well as national recognition in their fields of endeavor.

Sounds emanating through open windows of the stone house at 1217 Yewell Street, across from us included renditions of classic and popular music played on a piano by Paul "Chic" Olson, Professor and later Head of the Department of Economics at Iowa. He was a tall lanky man, always kind to the neighbor kids who crossed his lawn. Wife, Ruth and daughter Julie made up the rest of the family. Fond of the Olsons, the neighbors regretted, but tolerated, the yapping of their black cocker spaniel, Chloe.

Directly behind the Olsons at 1218 Friendly Avenue lived the poet, Paul Engle and his first wife, Mary. He wrote poetry in a small wood house annex, constructed in the backyard for him to work in quiet and privacy. Paul later became Iowa's Poet Laureate and Director of the famous Iowa Writers' Workshop—named by *US News & World Report* as the best in the United States—and he also directed The International Writers' Workshop with his second wife, Hualing.

Two artists lived next door to the Olsons in a white brick house at 1215 Yewell Street, Charles "Chuck" and Bobby Okerbloom. Bobby was a homemaker but had no children. She was slender, attractive with prominent eyes and a low-pitched sexy voice reminding one of Lauren Bacall. Chuck, a member of the art faculty at Iowa, was tall, erect with a pencil thin mustache resembling another movie actor, Errol Flynn. I might be standing in our front yard directly across the street, when unpredicted, the Okerbloom's front door would bang open as Bobby ran giggling out of the house, wrapped in a Cedar Rapids Country Club towel, Chuck in hot pursuit, embracing behind the shrubbery, creating a scene perfect for a current television advertisement of the remedy de jour for erectile dysfunction.

Chuck Okerbloom had a blue iris in one eye and a brown iris in the other. I have seen but one other person with a similar congenital anomaly. Chuck claimed one eye was a glass prosthesis, which after closing his eye, he would cover it with his handkerchief, pretend to extract and clean it on his trouser leg, then replace it, to the great amazement of his youthful audience congregated on his front steps to listen to his funny stories and admire his drawing. Sometimes, he would call to one of my playmates across the street, "Hey, Tom, do you want to earn a quarter?" To which, the little entrepreneur, running over breathlessly said, "Yes!" only to be deflated by Chuck's, "Well then, go earn it."

In 1942, when serious faces and talk replaced the smiles and levity of earlier years in our neighborhood, Chuck and Bobby, with somber expressions, spoke of Chuck's younger brother, a pilot and Major in the Army Air Force whose bomber squadron had been activated. Chuck, now in his late 30's, worked to resolve his ambivalence about war. After two weeks talking with Bobby and searching his soul, he seemed at peace. He enlisted in the US Army Air Corps and soon left for training at an airbase in Texas, and Bobby went to stay with her folks in Ohio.

Through Chuck's many letters to my parents and me—my mother encouraged me to write to servicemen—he told us of his promotion from Private to Corporal to Sergeant and of his assignment as a recruiter of women to the Air WACs (Woman Army Corps), duty station Dallas, Texas. On 28NOV1943, he wrote that his candidates were "broken- down riveters," whom he tried to convince would win the war as technicians, drivers, and mechanics. To relieve boredom, Chuck and his partner, both given to "corny jokes," he wrote, stocked the recruiting office with items from Magic Land, a nearby novelty store that sold exploding cigars, water spurting button-hole flowers, leaky water glasses, etc. A Colonel unexpectedly dropped in for a visit before Chuck could stow his items, and tested nearly every one of them, including lighting exploding matches and picking up an ashtray whose bottom fell out distributing ashes all over the desk. Apologizing for messing up Chuck's office, instead of pressing charges, the Colonel stepped outside, leaving Chuck convulsed with laughter under his desk. After judging an art show in Dallas, Chuck's next assignment, as ground crew, was Saipan. I remember seeing a photo in the newspaper of a painting he made there. I never found out if he watched another Iowan, Colonel Paul W. Tibbets, take off from Saipan in the B-29, Enola Gay, to release the atomic bomb over Hiroshima, leading to the end of World War II without the millions of military and civilian casualties anticipated with the planned invasion of the Japanese Islands. Returning home after the war, Chuck became Chairman of the Art Department, The University of Arkansas in Fayetteville.

Louise and Paul Risley and their two daughters, Barbara and Carol, lived in the next house north of the Okerblooms, 1213 Yewell Street. Barbara was my age and had mild asthma and eczema, both of which she outgrew to become a beautiful woman like her mother. Barbara and her sister played with Julie Olson, and occasionally they were included in boys' games. Mrs. Risley had a soft southern accent and hailed from Atlanta, I think. Dr. Risley had a small mustache like Chuck's and my father's. None of the men in this academic community cultivated beards. Before World War II, the Risleys moved to Eugene, Oregon, where Dr. Risley became Chairman of the Department of Zoology at The University of Oregon.

Sonya and Umberto Albrizio moved from New York City to their new home at 1223 Ginter Avenue, leaving an ultimate urban lifestyle to reside in our Moffitt neighborhood at the edge of an Iowa cornfield. Unlike all other dog owners in Iowa City, who permitted their pets total freedom to roam as they pleased, the Albrizios walked their toy poodle on a leash around the block after supper every evening, as they had on the sidewalks of New York. We had no sidewalks, and no one living on our street ever heard of a "pooper scooper." The neighbors excused the Albrizio's bizarre behavior, welcoming with affection this warm and engaging couple to their evening gatherings and parties. Sonya was the daughter of White Russian parents and a former ballerina. A couple of inches shorter than Sonya, Umberto, slender, swarthy, black hair and eyebrows, had a charming Italian accent and ebullient personality. I believe he fled fascist Italy, but I never knew when he came to America or why he picked our neighborhood in which to settle. However, he came to The University of Iowa to direct the sculpture program in the Art Department. I inherited a lovely piece of work that he made for my folks.

My father's colleague, Dr. James Greene, and his family lived across the street from the Albrizios at 1202 Yewell Street. His sons, Jimmy and George, were part of our kids' group. Years after Dr. Greene moved to Houston, Texas, as Chairman of the Department of Internal Medicine at Baylor, I met Jimmy in Chicago at the meetings of the Central Society for Clinical Research when I was on the faculty of The University of Chicago. After Harvard Medical School and postgraduate training, Jimmy became a nephrologist on the faculty of The University of Michigan. Except for retaining a Texas accent, acquired growing up in Houston, he had the same self-confidence and equanimity that I admired in him 20 years before. We renewed our friendship, making it a point to have lunch one day during subsequent annual meetings of the Society. Jim later opened, in Kalamazoo, Michigan, a private practice and operated a dialysis center for patients with kidney failure.

James Greene, Sr., wrote my father from Houston that he awoke one night, startled to find Margaret, his wife, not breathing and had no pulse. He rolled over, made a fist and struck her on the left side of her chest. That precordial thump, restarted her heart and saved her life, years before that action was codified in the guidelines for CPR (cardio-pulmonary resuscitation).

Arthur Blome, MD and his family lived next door south of the Greenes at 1206 Yewell Street. His son, Donny, was a year older than me. We became good friends, playing together for a couple of years until his father, in 1942, opened his private practice of Obstetrics & Gynecology in Ottumwa, Iowa. After a hiatus of seventy years, Don sent me a photograph of your humble, then five-year old author, replete with pointed paper hat and horn, grinning over cake with several other similarly attired neighborhood kids at Donny's dining table, celebrating his sixth birthday. A chance meeting of mutual friends in Arizona led to our reunion in Iowa

City with the mandatory tour of Don's and my old stamping grounds, Yewell and Grant streets.

Kenneth Brinkhouse, MD had moved with his family to 1210 Yewell Street before World War II. He was born in Elkader, Iowa, and died in Chapel Hill, North Carolina, in 2001, at the age of 92. He was a tall, slender, gentle man with brown hair who wore glasses and never aged in appearance during the many years that I knew him. Before the war, Dr. Brinkhouse was a junior member of a team of pathologists that included Drs. Walter Seegers and Emory Warner at The University of Iowa who were interested in the mechanisms of blood clotting. In their pioneer studies of blood coagulation, the Iowa group discovered Vitamin K and elucidated its critical role in hemostasis.

At the end of World War II, he returned to his Moffitt home on Yewell Street from service in the Army Medical Corps, but soon thereafter, Dr. Brinkhouse joined the medical faculty of the University of North Carolina in Chapel Hill. There he undertook studies with a colony of hemophilic dogs, identified anti-hemophilic factor (Factor VIII) in normal plasma, and devised replacement therapy with normal fresh-frozen human plasma to control hemorrhage in patients with hemophilia who lack Factor VIII in their blood. As Chairman of Pathology at North Carolina, he continued his research on blood clotting long after he retired, contributing to our better understanding of hemostasis. In addition to international recognition, he was elected to the National Academy of Sciences. He was always interested in news from Iowa when Karen and I breakfasted with him at the annual meetings of the American Society of Hematology.

Wilbur and Ellie Miller and their two sons Curt and Bruce, who were about my age, replaced the Brinkhouses at 1210 Yewell Street. Dr. Miller was a graduate of Amherst College and Harvard Medical School. He had a small thin mustache and resembled Nigel Bruce, the British actor who played the role of Dr. Watson in the early Sherlock Holmes movies. He was Professor and Head of the Department of Psychiatry and Director of The Iowa State Psychopathic Hospital across the street from University Hospitals. Ellie, a lovely woman with red hair and pink cheeks, a good friend of my mother's, was the daughter of a famous gunsmith named Roper. His custom-made pistol grips were sought by expert competition target shooters.

One of my 3-year old playmates, Tommy Tiffin, who lived next door at 1214 Yewell Street, contracted measles encephalitis. Its sequel consigned him to a mental institution for the rest of his life. It is hard to understand why some parents—despite numerous studies showing no etiologic relationship between immunizations and autism—deny their infants the benefit of immunization to prevent measles, polio, and other catastrophic diseases. Yet we cannot subscribe to the view of acerbic H. L. Mencken regarding those who eschew immunization. He was alleged to have said when told many citizens of New York opposed the use of small pox vaccination, "It would be good for the country, because the disease would kill off a lot of morons."

Jimmy Macy, a good friend, lived with his father, mother, and two sisters in a white clapboard Moffitt house just south of us across Friendly Avenue at 1302 Yewell Street. Jim's father Reuben "Red" Macy, was a tall robust sunburned man who had been raised on a farm near Sigourney, Iowa. He cultivated behind his home the largest, most productive and most beautiful vegetable garden in the neighborhood. Red Macy was the first Chief of the radiology technicians at University Hospitals. Irene, Jim's mom, was a sweet person who always went out of her way to welcome her children's playmates to her home. Jimmy obtained a degree in engineering and later managed the Sara Lee Confectionary Plant in New Hampton, Iowa.

The Butterfields lived across the street from the Macys on the southwest corner of Yewell and Friendly at 1301 Yewell Street. Mr. Butterfield was Principal at Longfellow Grade School where his imposing stature and black hair must have commanded respect and a disciplined response from his young charges. If most Longfellow students were intimidated by his presence, his twin sons, Tommy and Larry, never seemed to be. They were always in some kind of trouble for infractions of discipline, like throwing rocks or shooting B-B guns. But, when they were out of the "doghouse," they added excitement to all our activities—playing cowboys and Indians, cops and robbers, or war games.

Jacques and Helen Gottleib lived on the east side of Yewell in its 1400 block. They enjoyed good music and hosted the neighborhood's New Year's Eve Party, which children did not attend. Dr. Gottleib, a tall kind man, had the popular thin mustache. Mrs. Gottleib was tall with long tanned legs and arms. Large loose bracelets encircled her wrists. Carpooling with my father during the war, I got to ride in the rumble seat of Dr. Gottleib's Ford Model-A Roadster. They dropped me off at school on their way to work. Jacques Gottleib, MD was well known for his work on depression and other psychiatric illnesses. He was not a Freudian psychoanalyst. He left Iowa to become Chairman of Psychiatry at Wayne State University in Detroit, Michigan.

A former resident of the house at 1305 Yewell Street told me that it was the farmhouse that had belonged to the farmer who had sold his land in which Moffitt had planted his colony, encompassing his houses on Yewell Street, Ginter, Pickard, and Friendly. An internist colleague of my father's, Dr. Raymond Gregory, and his family lived in the house at 1305 Yewell during my first recollection. Before he left to assume the Chairmanship of Internal Medicine at The University of Texas-Galveston, he spent part of his last day at Iowa telling his departmental chairman what he thought of him, "a revolving S.O.B." Raymond and my dad were great friends, getting together every May in Atlantic City, New Jersey, for the annual meetings of the nation's premier clinical research societies. After giving a paper there one spring, I joined them in Dr. Gregory's hotel room where I nearly choked on their cigar smoke as they castigated politicians in academic medicine, to whom my father referred as "clinical dropouts." Dr. Gregory, a kind but crusty forthright man with large gnarled hands who loved to hunt wild game in Texas, said that when he left Iowa, he decided to become a subspecialist. He picked cardiology, because it was easiest to learn and took him only six weeks of study to qualify, he said. He built an excellent Department of Internal Medicine in Galveston.

Chapter V
Yoo-Hoo Yewell Street

Everyone on Yewell Street was welcome, and everyone knew everyone else; it was an inclusive society. I cannot recall any bad feelings, grudges, or feuds between our neighbors. When Karen and I lived on Chicago's south side, security was imperative, as it is in Iowa City today, but when I was growing up in our south side Moffitt neighborhood, no one locked the doors of his house or automobile. Emerging from washing dishes in the kitchen or from attending to personal hygiene in the bathroom, it was not unusual to find a neighbor standing in our living room, having entered without knocking, announcing herself to my mother with, "Yoo-Hoo, Laura." Although the practice must have occurred in other parts of Iowa City, a town of 15,000 people, some residents of other neighborhoods started calling our street, "Yoo-Hoo Yewell Street."

Boys and girls, their dogs yelping at their heels, ran freely all over the neighborhood, playing tag, hide and seek, kick the can, and king on the hill. Girls sometimes induced boys to jump rope or play hopscotch. Older kids played softball, touch or tackle football, or bicycle polo. Later, there were war games. Parents tolerated, but frowned upon, low level vandalism on Halloween—like ringing doorbells, soaping windows, and upending garbage cans. There were no instances of graffiti or property damage in our neighborhood, but in the Sunnyside Addition to the west, the prank in which an acquaintance detonated a dynamite cap under a privy while its fastidious owner was seated on the throne, might have caused serious physical injury rather than the indignity of the frightening counter-eruption from below. The perpetrator was apprehended, made to apologize, and grounded for his "terrorist" act.

Many faculty members sent their children to a nursery school (child care) operated by the University. This preschool convened in a lovely old three-story Victorian-style clapboard house with a Mansard roof. Located on the northeast corner of Capitol and Market streets, next door to the First Presbyterian Church, "Old Brick," the house was razed and replaced by the Pomerantz Center for Career Services Program. Most of my classmates in this "head start" program stayed together for the next 15 years, submitting to all sorts of measurements, and experiencing a unique educational opportunity in the Laboratory School; i.e., The University of Iowa Elementary and University High School. Some of us survivors met in October 2012 for our 60th Year U-High Reunion, greeting each other as if it was yesterday, and we were in school together again.

Men wearing straw cowboy hats and red bandannas strolled downtown, showing off beards cultivated to celebrate Iowa City's centennial in the summer of 1939. That was a banner year when City High School opened its doors on the east edge of town, "out in the country," people said. Who could predict 50 years later, it would be surrounded by homes and that one of its graduates, Tom Cech, would win the 1989 Nobel Prize for Chemistry for his discovery of the catalytic properties of RNA?

On another day that same year, a warm fall afternoon in 1939, I remember walking down Yewell Street. I could hear clearly the play-by-play broadcast of the Iowa-Notre Dame football game, emanating from every open window on the block, climaxing on the radio and by each resident who walked out on his porch to cheer as Nile Kinnick made the winning touchdown for the "Ironmen of '39."

Since 2005, the 14-foot bronze statue of Nile Kinnick at the south entrance of Kinnick Stadium memorializes him as the Heisman Trophy winner for 1939, carrying his jacket and books, acknowledging his achievements as class president, an honor student, and Navy flier. If he had survived service in WWII, many persons predicted he would be elected Governor of Iowa. As Kinnick's life was cut short when in 1942 his Navy plane crashed in the ocean, so was the life of his renowned sculptor, Larry Nowlan, who died of natural causes in Windsor, Vermont, at the young age of 48 years. Nowlan began the tradition, leading Iowa football players to touch the sculpted football helmet at Kinnick's feet for good luck as they entered the stadium for a game.

Another Iowan is memorialized by a bronze statue of a football player, posed as in the Heisman Trophy, at the entrance to the football field at Dubuque Senior High School. The school's alumnus, Jay Berwanger, won the first Heisman Trophy, graduating from The University of Chicago in 1936.

The eventual emigration of our talented Yewell Street neighbors represented a trend recapitulated by many persons, born, educated or who worked in Iowa and have left the state for greener pastures. Some who come to mind include: Presidents Herbert Hoover and Ronald Reagan—who as "Dutch" Reagan broadcast sports for WHO Des Moines, pollster George Gallup, agronomist and Nobel Laureate Norman Borlaug, Nobel Laureate Tom Cech, dramatist Tennessee Williams, bandleader Glen Miller, singer Andy Williams, Metropolitan Opera Singer Simon Estes, composer Meredith Willson, General Paul Tibbets, writers David Morrell (*First*

Blood, Rambo) and Robert Waller (*The Bridges of Madison County*), and actor Marion Robert Morrison (John Wayne).

Evenings Under the Elms

Summer evenings on Yewell Street were a "movable feast," not of food, but of meaty conversation. Without air conditioning in their homes, it was cooler outside, sitting in the shade of the elms enjoying a cool breeze until sunset. So after supper, the adults emerged from their houses, bringing their own chairs, to gather in a neighbor's front yard. The following evening they brought their hammock-like lawn chairs to another yard, the next day to another, so on down the block. These chairs, not aluminum or plastic, were made with a wide strip of green and white striped canvas tacked on both ends to a folding white wooden frame. You adjusted them for reclining by placing a round cross-bar into notches on either side of the supporting part of the frame. They were comfortable if they didn't collapse. However, the cross-bar had an unforgivable habit of slipping out of the well-worn notches, depositing the unsuspecting speaker on the grass in middle of a sentence, to his embarrassment and to his audience's delight.

This energy-efficient entertainment featured lively and humorous discussions of university, municipal, and national politics, and the state of the depressed economy. As the sunlight faded to dusk, streetlights and the glowing tobacco of pipes and cigarettes located the discussants while the kids, oblivious to the nature of the subjects under discussion, ran between the chairs, playing tag or catching fireflies. But with the rise to power of Mussolini and Hitler, the news from the gathering storm in Europe dominated the talk.

As faculty members of an academic institution, my parents and their friends must have had great concern to learn of the purge of "politically incorrect" anti-Nazi professors from the famous universities of Germany and Austria. On 3OCT1933, Nobel Laureate Ernest Lord Rutherford, the physicist who "split the atom" in 1932, chaired a meeting in London's Royal Albert Hall, attended by 10,000 people to raise funds for the relief of refugees, some 1,500 "non-Aryan" (Jewish) scientists dismissed from German universities and laboratories by May 1933. Rutherford introduced the main speaker, his old friend, colleague and Nobel Laureate, Albert Einstein, a refugee himself. Knowing that he could not return from a visit to the United States to work in Hitler's Third Reich, Einstein resigned from the Prussian Academy of Sciences. Planning to expel Einstein from the Academy on 1APR1933, a day set for the boycott of Jewish businesses, the Prussian Minister of Education, Bernhard Rust, instead sent Nazi thugs to ransack Einstein's home in Berlin.

September evenings remained warm, but the leaves of the elms on Yewell Street turned brown with the coming of fall, and sweaters began to appear. The children detected a serious tone in their parents' talk with the announcement on 2SEP1938 of Hitler's acquisition of the Sudetenland from Czechoslovakia. British Prime Minister Neville Chamberlain's reassurance that we would have "peace in our time," was viewed with skepticism then, appeasement now. More disturbing was news that on 9NOV1938 young Nazis went on a rampage in Berlin breaking the store windows (kristalnacht) of Jewish merchants, initiating a pogrom in which 90 Jews were killed at random and 20,000 to 30,000 sent to concentration camps.

Chapter VI
The Great Depression

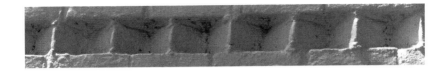

In Europe after World War I, reparation payments leading to staggering inflation, its industries devastated by four years of war, coupled with US persistent domestic wartime farm and industrial production, leading to great surpluses and manipulation of the stock market, contributed to cause the Great Depression, initiated in the United States with the stock market crash in October 1929. It is the height of irony and intellectual delusion to think that only seven months after taking office, President Herbert Hoover, whose unparalleled knowledge of foreign economies —gained from his former job as an international consulting mining engineer— whose service as Secretary of Commerce in the Harding and Coolidge Administrations assured his firm grasp of the domestic economy, who accurately predicted the depression, who begged unsuccessfully New York Governor Franklin Roosevelt to curb the abusive practices on Wall Street, was made a scapegoat and was blamed by his political opponents for starting a world-wide economic depression.

It calls to mind the blame laid on George Bush for the recent Great Recession. It resulted from policies initiated in the Carter Administration as the Community Reinvestment Act of 1977, the Community Development Act of 1992, and expanded by the Clinton Administration in 1999, designed to allow/force government controlled FNMA and FHLMC

(Fannie Mae and Freddie Mac) to issue mortgages to non-credible buyers, persons who had no ability to pay off their loans. The consequences of good intentions, providing a home for everyone, led to a home-building frenzy, a burst housing bubble, bankruptcies of lending institutions forced to make bad loans, a 187-billion dollar taxpayer bailout, home foreclosures, and a massive increase in bureaucracy, spending, and debt. Unemployment at the start of 2014 was still 7%.

In both economic disasters, government spending failed to significantly reduce unemployment. It wasn't until the end of World War II, when the only industry not bombed to smithereens, like those of Germany, Italy, Japan, France, and England, supplied the world with products grown or manufactured in the USA that its economy recovered and thrived during the administrations of Presidents Harry Truman and Dwight Eisenhower.

We are fortunate that citizens of the United States—despite the election of Franklin Roosevelt to an unprecedented four terms as president with his necessary government control of the economy to win World War II—never tolerated the imposition of a permanent totalitarian leader of a left-wing socialist regime like Joseph Stalin's Union of Soviet Socialist Republic (USSR) in Russia or like Adolph Hitler's National Socialist Party (Nazi) in Germany.

"The inherent vice of capitalism is the unequal sharing of blessings; the inherent virtue of socialism is the equal sharing of miseries."—Winston Churchill.

Married for five years, my father and mother could not afford to live together at the onset of the Great Depression. My dad, in training as a resident physician at Cleveland City Hospital, had a room in the Interns' Quarters while my mother, secretary to the cardiologist, Dr. Louis Katz at

St. Lukes Hospital across town, roomed with a girlfriend who also worked at the hospital. When I asked them, "How were you affected by the stock market crash initiating the Great Depression in 1929?" My father who had received room and board, but no salary from the hospital, and Mother who had a job, neither of whom owned stocks, an automobile, or had children to support, replied, "Not much."

You might wonder how it was living in Iowa City, a small Midwestern college community during the Great Depression (1929-1941)? With state support of the university, there was employment, but no high-paying jobs. Somehow residents, though relatively poor, had enough to eat without becoming obese. They bought groceries in small stores or farmers' markets, or grew their own vegetables, assuring their consumption of unprocessed organic food.

Banks that failed were replaced by new ones like The Iowa State Bank & Trust in 1934. Crops died in the heat and drought of the dust bowl 1930s without government support to prevent farm foreclosures, and most houses in town were of modest size with a one-car garage, unlike mansions on the outskirts of town today. Rents were relatively low. Houses on Burlington Street east of Summit and west of Muscatine had peeling paint from their sidings until the end of World War II. After the war, owners acquired funds for maintenance and remodeling, and now those homes, 80 years later, look attractive, much better than they did during the Depression, as I remember them.

Boys cut grass with push reel lawn mowers and weeds with sickles. Electric or gasoline powered lawn mowers, leaf blowers, weed eaters, hedge clippers, and chain saws, great labor-saving devices, would not rent the fabric of peace and quiet with their screeching motors for another 15 or 20 years. Fans served to cool bodies, somewhat, by evaporating sweat from perspiring skin in the summer, and without air conditioning to sustain a frenzied year-round work pace in July and August, life slowed down, and school didn't start until after Labor Day.

Without television, families and friends talked to each other, read newspapers and books, listened to the radio, records or attended movies at one of the five theaters within two blocks of each other downtown: Englert, Varsity, Iowa, Strand, and Pastime. Without smartphones, computers, Internet, social networking, or computer games there was no "digital dementia." There was no I.D. theft. Business telephones were answered by live persons who spoke English, and no huckster robo-calls rang at home. Broken appliances, "Made in the USA," were repaired, retained, and not discarded to be replaced by inferior foreign made products, sold with an optional supplemental extended warranty. There were no "recalls" of autos or products by the manufacturer. Public works like Hoover Dam, the Mississippi Lock and Dam System, and Lake MacBride State Park, provided men in the Civilian Conservation Corps and other programs with meaningful employment rather than welfare without work.

Instead of throwing away socks with holes in them, Mother darned socks, stretching them over a polished egg-shaped wooden device with a turned handle on one end, and she patched holes in the knees of corduroy trousers and the elbows of flannel shirts, permitting me to wear them without embarrassment. Conservation seemed a way of life during the Depression.

Prosecuted for murdering his wife, "Dusty" Rhodes was hung in Fort Madison, as a result of the only murder in Johnson County that I heard about during the Depression and World War II. Now assaults, robberies, and murders occur several times a year in Iowa City. Then, we rarely heard sirens of police cars, fire trucks, or ambulances like we hear every day now. Theft was rare, even in hard economic times, residents never locked their homes or automobiles, and the number of inmates in the county jail never exceeded its capacity.

Teachers taught students face-to-face without baby-sitting them in front of computers Bill Gates "altruistically" provided to be sure generations of adults would ensure an inexhaustible market for Microsoft products. Students graduated from high school with the ability to read, write, and compute without requiring remedial programs as freshmen in college. Despite the fiscal strains of the Depression, Iowa's literacy rate remained above 98%.

Health care for the indigent of the state was provided "free" by Iowa taxpayers at The University of Iowa Hospitals and Clinics in Iowa City and at Broadlawns Hospital in Des Moines before the inception of Medicare/Medicaid in 1965. With Medicare Part B paying 15-20% of an Iowa physician's bill in 2013, it is small wonder that a doctor paying off thousands of dollars in student loans, responsible for his or her nurse, receptionist, accountant, office manager, rent, astronomically high malpractice insurance premiums, and other expenses might choose to care for patients able to pay their bills. Already a shortage of primary care physicians creates concerns about the accessibility of medical care for a huge aging group of baby boomers facing cuts to Medicare to pay for the new government insurance initiatives. Electronic medical records (required by the Affordable Care Act), easily breached by hackers, has eliminated the relative privacy of the paper-based hospital chart, facilitating identity theft. These changes represent the consequences of government managed medicine.

Nobel Laureate, University of Chicago Professor of Economics, Milton Friedman said, "If you put the federal government in charge of the Sahara Desert, in five years there would be a shortage of sand."

During the Depression, patients with schizophrenia were cared for in County Homes and state facilities. After the advent of medicinal therapy for mental illness in the 1960's, those facilities were closed, patients discharged, outpatients stopped taking their drugs, homeless persons appeared on Iowa City sidewalks, the pedestrian mall, and street corners, a scene more familiar to my experience living in Chicago: the unintended consequences of good intentions. The Shelter House brings greatly needed temporary support for those seeking help to get back on their feet, but it does not serve as a center for rehabilitation of persons addicted to drugs. Perhaps for humanitarian reasons, long-term custodial facilities should be reconsidered.

Chapter VII
University Elementary School
1939-1946

Winter ice storms in the late 1930s coated tree limbs with ice, broke them and sent them crashing down on electrical power lines. Severed lines sparked and died, plunging Yewell Street into darkness. Candles lighted our rooms, and burning coal in our furnace warmed the house and kept water pipes from freezing. Snow drifts at the backdoor preserved food transferred from our electric refrigerator. After a week of this primitive living, which was fun at first, but then it became worrisome until the lights finally came on, all of us giving a sigh of relief. Amazingly, over 120 years of progress in electronic technology failed to prevent the loss of electrical power to hundreds of thousands of people, the East Coast victims of Super-storm Sandy on 29OCT2012.

Iowa's cold and snowy winters isolated our neighbors, limiting contacts to hailing each other across the street while shoveling snow from our driveways. The City rarely plowed Yewell Street. Model-A Fords and other autos with high suspensions of that era navigated well the ruts in the snow-filled street until the January and Spring thaws.

WAR IN EUROPE
During the fall of 1939, Father, when he returned home from work, usurped my monopoly of our Silvertone Radio in the late afternoon and

67

evenings, tuning it to reporters' H.B. Kaltenborn and Lowell Thomas news broadcasts of the war in Europe. This left me wondering how Jack Armstrong-The All-American Boy and the masked rider, Lone Ranger, coped with the fictional forces of evil. But the news revealed that the real evildoers were winning. In a blitzkrieg (lightning war), Adolf Hitler's Panzer Divisions invaded Poland on 1SEP1939, leading Great Britain to declare war on Germany on 3SEP1939. Warsaw fell to Hitler's Nazi armies on my father's 38th birthday, 27SEP1939. By then, the flags with the Nazi swastika flew over the capitols of Poland, Austria, and Czecho-slovakia.

A Tour of the East (21OCT-4NOV1939)

Anticipating that America might soon be dragged into war, my mother determined to take me at age 5 ½ years, to see her family in the East and attend the 1939 New York World's Fair. To my kindergarten teacher, Mother proposed that we take an educational trip to visit historic sites of America's birth. Miss Pegrom, my teacher, agreed to release me from a rigorous academic program: playing with building blocks, modeling with clay, finger painting, playing at recess, drinking chocolate milk, followed by taking naps on small rugs spread on the floor. She stipulated that I report to the class on my trip. I still have the scrapbook Mother annotated and we prepared to illustrate with postcards and photographs the details of this ambitious journey by auto and train covering 3,000 miles in 15 days.

The Rock Island Rocket

"Dick DeGruhn, Dick DeGruhn..." turned out to be me. More embarrassed by the notoriety than fearful the conductor, mispronouncing my name, would throw me off the train when he identified me, I mustered the courage to respond. He smiled and handed me a telegram. Words on strips pasted on yellow paper said:

"Iowa City, Iowa Oct.21, 1939

    Dick DeGowan (sic)

    Care Condr Rocket

    Have a good time, don't get lost.

    Ethan 10a"

Mother and I were but 45 minutes east of Iowa City on the gleaming new streamlined Rock Island Rocket when I received these words of bon voyage from our neighbor, Ethan Allen. We departed the Iowa City depot at 9:15 AM to arrive on time downtown at Chicago's LaSalle Street Station at 1:15 PM, exactly 4 hours later. Because the Rocket exceeded speeds of 120 miles per hour over the flat fields of Northern Illinois, actual travel time was only 3 hours 40 minutes. Ancient concessions won by the Railroad Brotherhood Union, which eventually helped kill passenger trains, mandated that train crews be replaced every 100 miles of travel, delaying us 20 minutes in Rock Island, Illinois, to accommodate changing the crew.

After crossing the Mississippi River at Davenport, Iowa, and our stop in Rock Island, we walked through the coaches to the Dining Car. There, black waiters in their white uniforms laid a sumptuous repast before us on white linen table cloths, adorned with a bud vase containing fresh flowers. Later, we reclined in brightly upholstered coach chairs, watching the beautiful countryside speed by. Contrast this luxurious travel at a cost of $5.00, seventy-five years ago, to flying today on a cramped airplane from our nearest terminal, The Eastern Iowa Airport in Cedar Rapids to Chicago's O'Hare Field. If there are no delays due to security checks, mechanical problems, flight cancellations for fog, thunderstorms or snow, the drive to Cedar Rapids, the flight and transportation to downtown Chicago requires at least 5 hours at a cost of several hundred dollars.

The Pennsylvania Railroad

Within 45 minutes of arriving in Chicago, we were seated in a coach of the Pennsylvania Railroad's Pacemaker-the World's Fair Special to New York City. Its advertising brochure boasted: a running time of 17 hours to Grand Central Station; air conditioned deluxe coaches with reclining seats reserved for the exclusive use of women with children; a Dining Car serving breakfast 50 cents, luncheon 65 cents, and dinner 75 cents on white linen table cloths; uniformed attendants who dim the lights at night and provide pillows at a moderate price; a commodious wash room and powder room with hot and cold running water, soap and towels; and magazines and radio in the Observation/Club Car. After viewing the beautiful Hudson River, at 8:00 AM the next morning we debarked into New York's bustling Grand Central Station. A Skyview taxi sped down 5th Avenue to deposit us at the Pennsylvania Station where Red Caps put us and our luggage aboard the Washingtonian, leaving for Philadelphia at 8:35 AM.

City of Brotherly Love

Mother's brother, Paul, a former general practitioner who was finishing his Residency in Radiology at Temple University, met us at North Philadelphia Station at 10:00 AM, 25 hours after we left Iowa City. After a fitful sleep on the train, I could barely stay awake. Paul drove us in his car to see the fall colors and the sites at historic Valley Forge, but I fell asleep and missed them. You might say George Washington and I slept there. Later, my Aunt Louise and Cousins Bill, Judy and Richard welcomed us to their home where we spent four enjoyable days with Uncle Paul's family.

Before leaving Philadelphia, we visited the Pennsylvania State House, now Independence Hall, where our Founding Fathers signed their suicide pact, the Declaration of Independence. A guard admonished me for touching the Liberty Bell. I told him it was cracked before I touched it, but years later his fellow Rangers of the National Park Service on Wednesday, 20FEB2002 armed themselves, heightening security in response to a threat to destroy the Liberty Bell. The inscription on the bell is from Leviticus 25:10 reads: "Proclaim LIBERTY throughout all the Land unto all the inhabitants thereof." Proceeding with our tour, we visited Old Christ Church where George Washington, John Adams, and Benjamin Franklin worshipped. From Franklin's grave, Mother purloined a sprig of ivy. On our return to Iowa City, she planted the ivy, which survived at our home for many years.

THE 1939 NEW YORK WORLD'S FAIR

At the brink of the second great catastrophe of the 20th Century, World War II, the 1939 New York World's Fair bolstered depressed spirits of the Great Depression, foretold a better future for America and show-cased New York City to the nation. As the first President of the United States, George Washington was inaugurated on 30APR1789 at Federal Hall in New York City, commemorated by his statue there and the opening of the World's Fair 150 years later. Its director, Grover Whalen, and the Fair's investors, having observed the financial success, despite the Depression, of Chicago's 1934 Century of Progress, hoped to emulate the Chicago fair's profits to the investors and the monetary contributions of the out-of-town visitors to the city's hotel, restaurant, and retail businesses.

Desperate to recruit exhibitors for the World's Fair from European countries, Director Grover Whalen sought an audience with Benito Mussolini. Whalen suffered a cold reception in Il Duce's palatial office, and when he asked Mussolini if Italy would construct an exhibit building at the Fair, the exchange was reported as:

"What, Italy compete with Wall Street?" the dictator responded;

"What would it accomplish?"

"The American people would like to know what fascism is," Whalen stated matter-of-factly.

Mussolini harrumphed. "You want to know what fascism is? It is like your New Deal!" (from Whalen, Grover: *Mr. New York: The Autobiography of Grover A. Whalen*, New York, G.P. Putnam's Sons, p. 186,1955.)

The Fair

Arriving in New York City at 12:00 noon, 26OCT1939, Mother wasted no time. We caught a shuttle train to the fairgrounds and toured the New York World's Fair for two hours. Scheduled to close its first year on Halloween 31OCT1939, we made it just in time to join the late surge of fairgoers, helping, but failing to approach predictions of the attendance necessary to turn a profit. The sparse attendance was a consequence of the war in Europe, and failed New Deal programs designed to end the Great Depression, ten years after the crash of the stock market on Wall Street in October of 1929.

Exhibits of technological innovation, like television, must have imbued fairgoers with optimism despite the persistence of a severe economic depression, but my only memories were of the Fair's gigantic art deco symbol, The Trilon and Perisphere, of an organ grinder and his red costumed monkey, and of Franklin Roosevelt's doting mother, pointed out by our guide as she attended the last day of the Fair before it closed. Ignoring my mother's call telling me it was time to leave, I tarried, reluctant to stop watching the antics of the organ grinder's monkey. Anxious that we not miss the train, she stepped out of sight in the crowd. Finding her dispelled my panic at being abandoned and ensured that I never dawdled when summoned again. We squeezed out the last minutes of sightseeing before boarding the Senator for New Haven, Connecticut, at 5:00 PM, climbing the back stairs to the open top of a double-decker bus at Penn Station in Manhattan and viewing the skyscrapers in a ride up 5th Avenue to 46th Street and back.

Uncle Ralph and Olive picked us up at 6:25 PM, 26OCT1939 in New Haven where mother's brother Ralph taught Neuroanatomy at Yale University School of Medicine. My cousin, Mary had been born in Amsterdam, The Netherlands the year before while Ralph was studying there on a Rockefeller Fellowship. The birth of their daughter on Holland soil conferred upon them Dutch citizenship, a policy devised by the government to tax fertile foreigners, and one currently followed in the United States to solicit votes of the immigrant parents crossing our southern border to give birth in American emergency rooms. I never found out how my aunt and uncle renounced their unwanted honor and tax liability.

CALEF FARM

My aunt and uncle drove us the next day, 27OCT1939, to Calef Farm, near Sanbornton, north of Concord, New Hampshire. Uncle Ralph and Olive had purchased this farm of more than 140 acres in 1938 for about $2,000. The farm house had been built in 1793, as President George Washington reluctantly began his second term of office. They loved their second home when Ralph worked at Yale and later for the National Cancer Institute in Bethesda, Maryland. Olive, an Iowan by birth, an easterner by choice, filled their home with antiques discovered in various places in New England. When Ralph retired as Deputy Director for Research at the Massachusetts General Hospital in Boston, they made it their principal and final home. It remains in the family, daughter Mary and husband Brian moved from Albuquerque to become residents of New Hampshire.

Ralph's mentor, Dr. Stone, and fellow Yale faculty members had purchased these old farms in neighboring hills for vacation homes during the Depression. Small hilly fields, fenced by long piles of big rocks, which previous owners had picked from the ground after they emerged from the spring thaw, bore little resemblance to Iowa cornfields. Boulder-filled fields gave silent testimony to the reason farmers crossed the Appalachian

Mountains to cultivate the rich black topsoil of the Ohio and Mississippi river valleys.

Memories, reinforced by retelling stories of our trip and subsequent visits, reminded me of Aunt Olive's kitchen, dominated by a black cast iron wood-fired cooking stove and a hand pump at the zinc kitchen sink. Large fireplaces with a central brick chimney and the stove heated this drafty old house on that cold late October day. Olive warmed the beds with an antique brass bed warmer containing hot coals from the fireplace before taking Cousin Mary from her playpen next to the stove and laying her in her crib in the bedroom. The next morning, Olive found that milk in bottles, delivered to the front porch, had frozen pushing the cardboard caps two inches high on a column of frozen cream. When the sun came out and temperatures rose, Ralph's kindly neighbor gave me my first horseback ride on the broad back of his docile plow horse. Despite his slow lumbering pace, it was a great thrill for this 5 ½ year old boy.

We left New England to visit Mother's older sister, Francis, her husband Lloyd and Cousins Carol and Hildegard in Farmington, Michigan. Then after seeing Granddad in Kalamazoo, Michigan, we rode the Michigan Central to Chicago. Departing Chicago's LaSalle Street Station on the Rock Island Rocket at 5:45 PM we were met in Iowa City by my father four hours later at 9:40 PM on 4NOV1939.

My mother noted all of these times and dates on our trip for our report to my kindergarten class and for our scrapbook. I list them here to show how easy and predictable traveling by train by a mother and a small child was seventy-five years ago. Astonishingly, it has taken over 60 years of highway gridlock, airline delays, and flight cancellations for government officials to consider restoring passenger train service to Iowa City and Des Moines, and still its future remains in doubt.

Chapter VIII
First Grade 1940-1941

Iowa's teachers—working in one-room rural and larger schools during the fall of 1940 when I entered First Grade of The University of Iowa Elementary School, the students, and their parents—deserve congratulations for the state's 99% literacy rate. My classmates and I were assigned to groups based upon test results of our reading ability. As our work with spelling and phonics helped us to improve our reading skills, we were promoted from one group to the next, robins to blue birds to the most advanced, cardinals.

Enjoying the ability to read for work and pleasure makes it hard for me to conceive how embarrassing it must be for an illiterate individual to depend upon literate persons for information with which to make important decisions. Unprincipled purveyors of information find it easy to take advantage of those so handicapped. My father, who read to me and who loved to read about science, history, and biography, asserted that those persons who could learn from what they read were not required to repeat the mistakes and experiments described by their predecessors but could move on from the point where the authors concluded.

President George W. Bush's campaign to reverse the trend toward functional illiteracy by assuring that every child in America was able to read by the Fourth Grade, is essential if our citizens expect to benefit from America's many opportunities. It is mandatory if we are to fulfill our responsibilities as enlightened citizens in the voting booth. Many, if not all, teachers voted against Bush for President and attacked his innovative No Child Left Behind program of standardized testing shortly after its inception, claiming it was counterproductive and unnecessary. Now, over 10 years later, New York students in grades 3-8 failed to meet or exceed the proficiency in 2012 for reading (31%) and math (31%) in the state's first round of testing under the new Common Core Standards, according to the New York State Education Department (*USA TODAY*, THURS, 8AUG2013).

State laws in the antebellum South prohibited slave owners from teaching their black slaves to read or write, keeping them illiterate, ensuring their dependency and inability to find more than menial employment if they escaped from their masters. Abraham Lincoln's Emancipation Proclamation, followed by the 13th Amendment to the Constitution, freed the slaves who then aggressively sought education in their churches, also banned before the Civil War, to guarantee their freedom from dependency. Currently, African-American students score below Hispanic, White, and Asian students on standardized tests. Besides redistricting school boundaries and bussing to achieve diversity of the student body—resulting in teaching to the lowest common denominator in a class or cruelly demanding that a student keep up with peers when he is unable—what solution have educators proposed to correct this disparity?

My teachers emphasized learning how to look up information rather than memorizing facts, as John Dewey proposed in his book, *The School in Society*, advocating "progressive education." Reflecting on an education where the student doesn't know anything, I prefer a modified paradigm for learning in which facts are memorized within a coherent structure like bricks in a building. When newly discovered data refutes a fact, the student with an open mind will replace the old "brick" with a new "brick" of information, retaining or altering the structure as indicated. In this situation, the student will have undergone an emotional "A Hah!" moment, facilitating his or her memory of the amended information. Anyway, one has to know something in order to look it up, and what does one do if the battery dies and electrical power is not immediately at hand for current technology?

One of the girls who joined our First Grade Class in September 1940 had to walk but three blocks to school. Mary Sue had come with her family from Evanston, Illinois, to live in the President's Mansion on Church Street. Her father, Virgil Hancher, an Iowa alumnus, arrived in Iowa City with impressive credentials: a doctorate in law, a Rhodes Scholarship, and former Dean of Law at Northwestern University. He served a long and distinguished tenure (1940-1964) as President of The University of Iowa during the war years of the 1940's and afterwards. He was the main speaker at our University High School graduation in which he mentioned that he may not have met us personally, but he had known we had been in his house, because food in his refrigerator mysteriously disappeared when Mary's friends visited her. Hancher Auditorium, named for him, brought class acts to the university and surrounding communities for 40 years until flooding of the Iowa River closed it in 2008. Rebuilt on higher ground, our community looks forward to the resumption of outstanding programing in Hancher's new home.

PRELUDE TO WAR

Opinions differed about how England and America should respond to the growing crisis in Europe before World War II. Enamored with Herman Goering's air force (Luftwaffe) as well as with his bride-to-be, the twice-divorced American, Mrs. Wallis Simpson, who received roses regularly from

Goering, Edward VIII of England was "encouraged" to abdicate as King in 1936. Americans Henry Ford, Charles Lindbergh, and the United States Ambassador to England, Joseph Kennedy, voiced opposition to American involvement and even spoke positively of Hitler's regime. However, President Roosevelt activated Selective Service on 29OCT1940, drafting young men for one year's service during peacetime. He traded with the British, aging destroyers for naval bases in the Caribbean. Later, Roosevelt introduced Lend Lease, sending to Britain essential goods, including rifles, through Atlantic waters infested with German submarines (U-boats). Critics claimed that using US naval vessels to convoy our cargo ships would indeed violate our neutrality; provoke U-boat attacks and lead to war with Germany. It did.

The Battle of Britain

On the day before my sixth birthday, 13MAY1940, Prime Minister Winston Churchill pledged the British to defend their island homeland and the Free World with, "blood, toil, tears and sweat," later abbreviated to "blood, sweat and tears." Two weeks later the BBC, on 26MAY1940, announced that Hitler's armies had defeated Allied Troops leading to their evacuation from Dunkirk, under fire from German fighters and dive bombers. In 10 days ships of the Royal Navy and an armada of small English watercraft removed 340,000 men from the beaches of France. Paris fell to the Wehrmacht on 14JUN1940, giving Nazi Germany control of Western Europe.

The Luftwaffe of ReichsMarshall Herman Goering bombed the cities of London, Manchester, and Liverpool during the summer and fall of 1940, The Battle of Britain. But England's new secret weapon, radar—a palindrome meaning "radio detecting and ranging"—warned the Royal Air Force (RAF) of approaching German planes as they crossed the English Channel. Jaunty RAF pilots, in response to wailing air raid sirens, scrambled into Spitfires to engage enemy bombers and fighters in dog-fights, shooting down 185 German airplanes one day. Acknowledging the courageous RAF pilots who thwarted invasion and stiffened the resolve to keep fighting, Churchill said, "Never have so many owed so much to so few."

Chapter IX
Banking Blood

Bleeding from battlefield wounds loses red blood cells that carry oxygen from the lungs to cells in the peripheral tissues, which require oxygen to metabolize glucose (sugar), producing energy to maintain the integrity of the cells. Without oxygen, cells die, blood pressure collapses, and death ensues; the lethality of hemorrhagic shock.

Results of studies by Karl Landsteiner and others, in the early part of the 20th Century, demonstrated the existence of red blood cell type agglutinins (A,B,O, & AB), permitting successful transfusion of fresh blood to prevent hemorrhagic shock, saving lives. In those early days, person-to-person direct transfusion required that donor and recipient patient were found immunologically compatible by blood typing and that they lie next to each other during the infusion of blood, impractical to implement under conditions in the front lines, or in the bombed-out neighborhoods of London during the blitz.

Collecting donor blood in sodium citrate solution prevented red cells from clumping or clotting allowing transfusions for a short time; not requiring the donor and recipient in the same room. Two American physicians, Oswald H. Robertson, MD, working with Peyton Rous, MD in his laboratory at the Rockefeller Institute, discovered that adding dextrose (sugar) to a suspension of red blood cells in citrate solution preserved blood long enough for Robertson to establish the first blood bank when he served in the British Army in World War I. Results of their studies and Robertson's wartime experience were published in the *British Medical Journal* in 1918.

Peyton Rous wrote to my father on 4APR1940, congratulating him on his work greatly improving the citrate-dextrose method of blood preservation, urging him to disseminate reprints of his papers among physicians in England and France who had forgotten about the work that he and Robertson published at the end of World War I. A long and cordial correspondence between Dr. Rous and my father ensued. In 1966, Peyton Rous was awarded the Nobel Prize in Medicine for his work on the viral etiology of cancer, shared with one of my teachers in medical school, Charles B. Huggins, MD.

My immersion in hematologic research began at the age of 6 years when I accompanied Father to the Iowa City Airport in the fall of 1940. We went there to meet the scheduled arrival of a United Airlines Flight, a DC-3, then on the mainline between New York and San Francisco. Was I there to participate in an historical research event, to help carry a gray wooden ice chest packed with ice-covered bottles of whole blood preserved in "DeGowin Solution," or to open the doors while Dad carried the chest into the terminal? I was never quite sure. The next day, we retrieved the gray chest at the airport after its 4,000 mile round trip from Iowa City to San Francisco, discovering as we peered inside, that much of the ice had melted, but the solution suspending the red cells was not red from their leakage of hemoglobin. Later analysis in my father's laboratory at University Hospitals showed that no hemolysis (destruction of blood) had occurred and that the red blood cells survived normally when transfused.

The Research

To protect the recipient of preserved blood from adverse consequences, my father, Elmer DeGowin, and his colleagues proved by their studies that stored blood was as safe and as effective as fresh blood transfused person-to-person. Blood was drawn from healthy donors into a citrate-dextrose solution contained in sterile glass bottles. Citrate prevented clotting of red blood cells, dextrose provided the substrate for red blood cellular metabolism to extend their life span, and refrigeration slowed metabolic enzyme degradation. Results of their studies at Iowa showed that whole blood could be stored safely for 21 days, setting the standard for the shelf-life of bank blood.

Prior to these and other experiments, many doctors thought that blood had to be transfused at body temperature to survive in the recipient's blood stream, that cold blood from refrigeration caused fevers and other reactions and that it could not be transported safely without being destroyed by sloshing around in its containers. They knew that shaking a bottle of dog's blood induced hemolysis, increased mechanical fragility. They did not know that a dog's red blood cells were much more fragile than that of human red cells. So with the onset of Nazi aggression in Europe and the anticipation that America would be forced to enter World War II, results of these studies assumed greater importance, demonstrating that blood donated in the United States could be flown to Great Britain and stored for the transfusion of soldiers to prevent hemorrhagic shock from battlefield wounds.

The Blood Bank

Bernard Fantus started the first civilian blood bank at Cook County Hospital in Chicago in 1936; (Fantus, B.: The therapy of Cook County Hospital: blood preservation, *J.A.M.A.* 109:128, 1937). However, blood was "preserved" for only 3-4 days, because Fantus used citrate solution without dextrose, which only prevents clotting of red cells. During his visit in 1938, my father was shown the blood bank at Cook County Hospital by its Director, Dr. Lindon Seed, a prominent Chicago surgeon. Returning to Iowa City, my dad established the Transfusion Service in 1938 and the Blood Bank at University Hospitals in February 1939. Later that year, his exhibit on the preservation of blood, using the improved citrate-dextrose method, at the annual meeting of the American Medical Association in St. Louis was recognized with the award of a gold medal to him and his coworkers.

Dr. Lindon Seed telephoned me in 1980 after my father's death, expressing his condolences and requesting material, for a museum exhibit, that my father might have collected about the history of blood banking. Dr. Seed told me that the Blood Bank at Iowa was the longest continuously operating one in the United States; the Cook County Supervisors had not always supported the operation of the blood bank at Cook County Hospital. Coincidentally, I knew Dr. Seed's son, Randy, in the class (UC'60) behind me in medical school, because we shared a generous faculty advisor, Dr. Henry T. Ricketts, who hosted a dinner for his advisees in his home every year.

The Dedication

At a dedication, 2:00 PM on 11DEC1981 in the Medical Alumni Auditorium, a year after my father died, the Blood Bank at The University of Iowa Hospitals was named Elmer L. DeGowin, M.D. Memorial Blood Center. His colleagues and friends gathered to pay tribute to his work, remarks I wish that he could have heard. He was a modest man; he did not subscribe to his former Chief, Bill Bean's 11th Beatitude, "If you don't blow your own horn, no one else will." His coworkers remarked that my father never wanted them to call the blood preservation fluid they developed, "DeGowin's Solution," like his friend Dr. John Alsever had "Alsever's Solution" attached to his preparation.

John W. Colloton, Director of The University of Iowa Hospitals and Clinics presented a bronze plaque to be affixed to the entrance of the blood center. Its inscription read:

> Dr. Elmer DeGowin, Professor, Department of Internal Medicine, Founded the University of Iowa Transfusion Service in 1938 and the Blood Bank in 1939 and served as its Director until 1966. The techniques he developed for the preservation, storage and transportation of human blood form the basis of modern blood banking and transfusion.

Francois M. Abboud, MD. Professor and Head, Department of Internal Medicine and President of the nation's premier clinical research society, The Association of American Physicians, pointed out that Elmer's US Army Contract represented the first research grant in the Department.

Robert C. Hardin, MD, my father's former medical resident, spoke of the "Early History of Blood Banking at Iowa;" he had worked in the laboratory to extend the life span of stored blood. Later, he was quoted, "DeGowin was the moving force that did this work. Although I did a lot of the work, the ideas were DeGowin's. I was a super technician."

After enlisting in the Army, in 1940-1941, Bob Hardin trained men in the medical unit of the Iowa National Guard based in Iowa City in the techniques of acquisition, storage, transportation, and administration of whole blood. Bob, a 28-year old Major in the US Army, supervised 500 personnel in England and France as the medical officer in charge of the Whole Blood Transfusion Program for the European Theater of Operations, before, during and after D-Day, 6JUN1944. Bob returned to Iowa after the war, wanted nothing to do with blood transfusion, specialized in endocrinology, became President of the American Diabetes Association, Dean of the College of Medicine, and Vice-President for Health Sciences. The Hardin Health Science Library is named for him.

Among other good friends who spoke at the dedication, was our editor, Joan C. Zulch, Editor of Medical Books Division of Macmillan Publishing Company of New York and London. She announced that the current 3rd edition of *Bedside Diagnostic Examination* by DeGowin and DeGowin had been adopted by every medical school in the United States, half of the Canadian schools, Physician Assistant's Programs, schools of Nursing, and schools of Osteopathy and Chiropractic. By that time, it had been translated into German, French, Italian, Spanish, and Greek.

Chapter X
Second Grade 1941-1942

American Indians became "Native Americans" years after I was taught about their culture in the Second Grade. As my ancestors were immigrants to North America in the 17th and 18th Centuries, theirs came earlier from Siberia over the Bering Strait. Have you wondered how the term "Native American" was selected to politically identify a group for special treatment instead of "Siberian-American?"

INDIAN CULTURE

A teepee erected in the back of our second grade class room served to focus our learning about nomadic Plains Indians, who seemed to enjoy an idyllic perpetual camping trip, true environmentalists, using all parts of the butchered American Bison for shelter, clothing, and food. Deprived of buffalo by white hunters and resistant to change from a stone-age hunter-gatherer, warrior society to an agrarian society, Indians lost out to Anglo-American hegemony, as Pat Buchanan opined, a consequence of a lax immigration policy and a failure to secure the borders.

Later, I learned more of Indian culture, replacing some schoolbook myths depicting Indians as ultimate conservationists, by reading accounts describing how Indians stampeded whole herds of bison off cliffs rather than culling the herd for the small number of beasts required for sustenance.

They killed hundreds of buffalo and deer, trapped beaver and fox in the Mississippi River Valley, not for personal consumption, but to trade their pelts for white man's goods, including whiskey. Apaches on reservations bridled at the 4th Calvary's Colonel Ranald MacKenzie's order that they refrain from beating their hard-working wives, asserting that he had no right to interfere with their culture. Chief Quanah Parker refused to give up the Comanche tradition of polygamy, having at one time 7 wives and 19 children.

My mother's ancestors, who survived the 1694 Oyster River Indian Massacres in New Hampshire, and later attacks encouraged by the French, wrote that after their homes were burned, their wives and children were carried to Canada and held for ransom. Indian warriors, who feared the crying of babies would alert pursuers, grabbed the infants by their ankles and bashed out their brains against a tree.

Finally, Indians fought on the side of the British against Americans during the Revolutionary War and during the War of 1812, and on the side of the Confederates during the American Civil War. Despite the fact they lost, fighting on the losing side in each instance, the US taxpayer continues to support their descendants. Hopefully, embracing capitalism, by managing gambling casinos, with profits going to tribes for improved health care and education, may facilitate an end to dependency in some of the reservations. In my view, the best outcome would be for Indians to retain pride in their heritage and simply become American citizens, like the rest of us immigrants from diverse ethnicities and cultures.

DECEMBER 7, 1941

Mary Jane Baker was the only member of our Second Grade Class who, on Monday, 8DEC1941, had not heard that the Japanese had bombed the US Naval Base at Pearl Harbor. I've wondered if her parents, Tillie and

Professor Joe Baker, kept the news from her or did not know it. The rest of us knew what had happened the day before.

Our class listened intently to the radio, which Miss Hyslip, our teacher, had brought to school that Monday morning, while President Roosevelt declared that the Japanese sneak attack on December 7th was, "a day that will live in infamy." With over 3,000 of our servicemen killed, our Pacific Fleet devastated, and our shores threatened by Japanese and German submarines, war came to the America. My grade school years spanned those of World War II (WWII), during which I learned how to read, write, and calculate. From my parents, teachers, the radio, newspapers, and movie newsreels of starved refugees and bombed out cities, I learned the difference between good and evil.

THIRD GRADE (1942-1943)
After returning from a field trip to the Iowa City Park, where we visited a restored pioneer's log cabin, members of our Third Grade Class undertook domestic chores of pioneer women. We made tallow candles and lye soap, carded wool, spun flax to make thread, and prepared food for winter storage, drying sliced apple rings, and making beef jerky. More useful, I learned the multiplication tables, a memorized set of facts I've used every day of my life.

Friends attending the Catholic schools, St. Mary's or St. Patrick's, drilled for hours, filling notebook pages with looping "l's" and rounded "O's," until their beautiful, legible, cursive Palmer-method handwriting flowed freely on the paper. I envy them for their handwriting skills. Attending my so-called "progressive" school had its shortcomings in that department. Our regimen was to spend a little time shaping our letters, like those posted on cards above the blackboard, and then to write as fast as we could in the allotted time: "Fourscore and seven years ago our fathers brought forth upon this continent a new nation, conceived in liberty and dedicated to the proposition that all men are created equal. Now we are engaged in a great civil war testing whether that nation or any other nation so conceived and so dedicated can long endure." Although I memorized the first two lines of Lincoln's Gettysburg Address, which are very meaningful to me, I have struggled threescore and ten to write legible school themes, personal letters, notes on patient's charts, and on prescription pads. A tribute to my partial success came one day when a pharmacist asked one of my patients whether a doctor had written his prescription, because the pharmacist said he could read it.

Several School Board members in 2013 advocated discontinuing the teaching of cursive writing, a mistake in my view. Not only will students be unable to read historic documents, but cursive writing is very personal, brain-to-hand pen-to-paper, as distinctive as a person's speech. Compared to printing by hand, handwriting can be written faster and is more difficult to forge than printing.

Mother and Shorty, Summer 1933, at 1312 Muscatine Ave.

1218 Yewell Street. Uncle Ralph, Mother, and Father.

Don Blome's 6th birthday party.

War games: Larry Butterfield, author, Keith Jones, and Tommy Butterfield. Yewell Street.

Dog Chum, and coonskin cap were gifts from the Cumiskeys to the author. 1218 Yewell Street.

Cousin Bill, John Carney, and Dotty Carney. Lawn Chairs on Yewell Street

Mother and Dog Chum before she left for the farm. Note the quarantine sign under the mailbox.

Vacant lot and window box, 1218 Yewell Street

Julie Olson and Barbara Risley, Yewell Street

Larry Butterfield, Donny Blome, Tommy Butterfield, Yewell Street

1215 Yewell Street

Chuck and Bobby Okerbloom, 1215 Yewell Street

Private Chuck Okerbloom, US Army Air Corps, Texas, 1943

Professors Megrew, Okerbloom Return To Art Department

Prof. Alden Megrew and Prof. Charles I. Okerbloom, both recently returned to the university to resume their positions on the art department faculty.

Professor Okerbloom, who left the university in October, 1942, to enter the army, served as a sergeant in the army air corps for three years. He was stationed on Saipan with the 73rd bomb wing for 16 months.

After receiving a B. A. degree from Ohio State university in 1930, Professor Okerbloom came to the university in 1934 and received an M.A. degree here in 1938. He teaches courses in water color painting and drawing.

Professor Megrew, who left the university in March, 1943, served as a lieutenant in the naval air corps for 34 months. For 14 months he was stationed in the Pacific and Caribbean theaters. Coming here from Harvard university in 1940, Professor Megrew was on the staff for three years before entering the service. He teaches a course in the history of art.

Professor Megrew's wife and daughter, Anne, live at 1305 Yewell street. Professor Okerbloom and his wife plan to resume their residence at 1215 Yewell street in the near future.

97

Lt. Frank S. (Red) Cumiskey, Lafayette, Indiana

U.S.S. Coral Sea
7th Flt. P.O.
San Francisco

LIEUTENANT FRANK S. CUMISKEY
USNR

March 27, 1944

Dear Elmer, Laura & Dick:

I received your letter some time ago and I'm terribly sorry for waiting this long to answer it and I assure you I will try to do much better in the future. I imagine about this time of the year you are planning your garden and getting set for another grand summer in Iowa City. I shall never forget that summer I spent there and especially the wonderful people on Yewell St.

Laura it seems you must be the family correspondent with the men folk all keeping so busy. I think that's a good idea because I have always thought that women could do more justice to a letter than men. Women seem to be better posted on the good old scuttlebutt than men so keep writing I enjoy your letters very much.

By this time I assume that Chum has returned and I hope alone. Chum is really

Three page letter from Red Cumiskey on board the USS Coral Sea, 1944

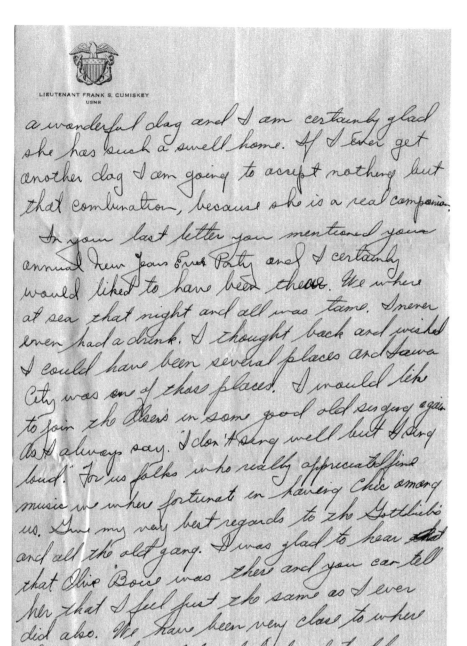

LIEUTENANT FRANK S. CUMISKEY
USNR

a wonderful dog and I am certainly glad
she has such a swell home. If I ever get
another dog I am going to accept nothing but
that combination, because she is a real companion.
In your last letter you mentioned your
annual New Years Eve Party and I certainly
would liked to have been there. We where
at sea that night and all was tame. I never
even had a drink. I thought back and wished
I could have been several places and Iowa
City was one of those places. I would like
to join the Olsen's in some good old singing again
as I always say. "I don't sing well but I sing
loud." For us folks who really appreciate fine
music we where fortunate in having Chic among
us. Give my very best regards to the Gottlieb's
and all the old gang. I was glad to hear
that Olive Bowie was there and you can tell
her that I feel just the same as I ever
did also. We have been very close to where
her husband is stationed but unfortunately

we get very little time to spend ashore
down here because of regulations and
also because of our activities. We have been
extremely busy and at time somewhat discouraging
but has been interesting. I mentioned in my last letter
I would like to go once more and then come home
well heres whats happened. We have been on
several pushes since than and the future seems
to be getting blacker as far as getting home is concerned.

I am enclosing a sheet of paper for Dick to
put in his scrap book. I picked this up
ashore and as far as I can make out its a sheet
out of a Jap's supply officers books. Maybe someone around Jewell street can decipher it. Although
theres lots of things available most of them are
not mailable.

I hear from Betty often. She is in Florida
and seems very happy and likes her work very
much.

Give my regards to everyone and do writ
soon,

Red

ONE OF 6 NEW STREAMLINED ROCK ISLAND ROCKETS

Rock Island Rocket

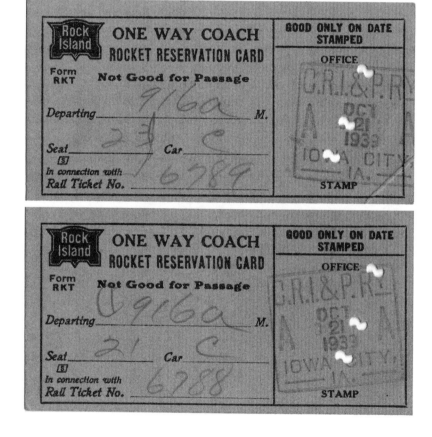

New York World's Fair, 1939

Major Robert C, Hardin, MD, 1218 Yewell Street.

THE ROCKEFELLER INSTITUTE
FOR MEDICAL RESEARCH
66TH STREET AND YORK AVENUE
NEW YORK

April 4, 1940

Dear Dr. deGowin:

Some time ago O. H. Robertson wrote the news that you had improved the citrate-dextrose method of blood preservation, and I have been looking forward eagerly to your papers. They are all that one could hope, and they should save many a life if the Allies will only take notice of them. There's the rub! The isolation of the English, not to speak of the French, in some scientific matters that immediately concern them is sometimes remarkable.

Last autumn it became evident, through the English literature, that the directors of blood transfusion stations were proceeding from scratch, using the ancient citrate method as if no other was available. I felt it to be a duty to bring the citrate-dextrose method to their attention and hence had our papers reprinted, together with Robertson's, and mailed them to all and sundry in England and France. Gye, of the Imperial Cancer Research Fund, on receiving the reprints wrote: "I have sent your reprints to the various people in charge of transfusions, civil and military, and judging by letters it is quite certain that the hardly won knowledge of the last war had been forgotten."

Now your new method supersedes ours, and the Europeans should know of it as soon as possible. It might take months or a year or two in the ordinary event. Why not make use of the list I have compiled of foreign workers on transfusion and send your papers to every one of them? In special it would be good to send reprints to Sir Henry Dale of the Medical Research Council, to Dr. W. E. Gye, Imperial Cancer Research Fund, Burtonhole Lane, The Ridgeway, Mill Hill, London, N.W.7, and to Dr. Alexis Carrel, Ministry of Health, Paris. Carrel has taken on the job of improving the transfusion service in France. Come to think of the matter, though, you may have a more comprehensive list than my own. Please don't forget to send me the reprints too.

With congratulations on a greatly needed achievement,

Sincerely yours,

Peyton Rous

Dr. E. L. deGowin
College of Medicine
State University of Iowa
Iowa City, Iowa

105

Capt. Moyers to Talk At Meeting Tonight For All SUI Men

10/9/45

Capt. Robert Moyers

★ ★ ★

Capt. Robert E. Moyers, 1942 graduate of the university, will be the principal speaker at the all-university meeting for men in the river room of Iowa Union at 7:45 tonight.

Captain Moyers participated in the battle of Sicily in July and August, 1943, as a member of a mobile surgical team with the British Eigth army. After this, he started his training for a position as an allied medical officer in Greece. In this capacity he was in charge of the organization of medical service, getting medical supplies into Greece, training medical corpsmen, and establishing new hospitals throughout the country. Captain Moyers assisted in over 250 major battlefield operations.

Established Housing

Before the liberation of Greece, he directed the establishment of a system of soup kitchens, hospitals and temporary housing for over 100,000 people in the devastated area which the Germans had just abandoned. This job was done in less than six weeks.

After the liberation of Greece, Captain Moyers was influential in bringing about the peace negotiations which concluded the Greek civil war.

He has received more decorations than any other dentist in the history of the United States Army, being decorated five times by the American government, twice by the British, and twice by the government of Greece. He was also the youngest captain ever commissioned in the medical department.

Taking Graduate Work

At present, he is here taking graduate work in orthodontics and is a member of the staff in that department.

Capt. Robert Moyers Tells of Greek Action At Men's Meeting

Expressing the greatest admiration for Greek guerrillas and their unceasing efforts against the aggressors in their native land, Capt. Robert Moyers, a graduate of the University of Iowa, spoke at a meeting of all-university men sponsored by the Y.M.C.A in the river room of Iowa Union last night.

Moyers volunteered for overseas duty when he went into the army. Eighteen days later he was on his way.

"That taught me not to volunteer," he said.

Landing in Sicily in July of '43, he went from there to Cairo and then on to Greece, where he stayed for 18 months. Attached to the dental corps, much of his work consisted of establishing hospitals, dropping supplies, and teaching the use of new drugs to medical men in the back country.

"It has always been characteristic of the country," he remarked, "that whenever danger threatens, the people take to the hills."

This time it was the same. Moyers had the opportunity to see what it meant. Rocky terrain, rising above the sea; trails not wide enough to accommodate a jeep; paths so steep and narrow that there were only upper and lower forks, never right or left. In this country the guerrillas lived and fought.

Moyers described several incidents which he hopes never to have to witness again, among them scenes of wounded without adequate hospital facilities or doctors. He described his feeling of utter helplessness in his lack of preparation for that sort of thing.

"There was a sergeant in my outfit of whom I was really proud," he said. The sergeant located typhus in an isolated mountain village and reported to Captain Moyers. Contact was made immediately with Italy to send out medical supplies to ward off an epidemic. The village was sprayed with DDT and other precautions were taken to prevent any more cases of the dread disease. From that tiny village, the whole of Greece might have been caught in a plague similar to those reported in history. But that sergeant was on the lookout for it and prevented it.

Explaining how well the Americans and the Greeks got along, Moyers told of the incident in which students at an American college in Athens, upon hearing there were Americans in the hills, left their studies and homes to join them. They sacrificed a great deal, jeopardizing their safety and the safety of their families to fight on the side of right as they saw it.

There were humorous incidents along with the serious ones. There was the time in Athens when it was almost impossible to get through. Moyers said the soldiers draped an American flag across the front of a jeep, strung one along the back, and singing the "Star-Spangled Banner" loudly, drove their way through the milling mob.

"Incidentally," Moyers remarked "the 250 operations mentioned in the papers couldn't have been military. They must have been surgical. I couldn't have stood so many."

Capt. Moyers was introduced by Jack Fickel, M2 of Henderson, president of the Y.M.C.A.

106

Uncle Ed, OSS, and Uncle George, US Congress

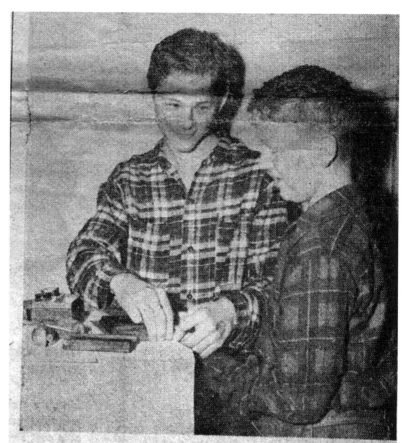

Spark plug of the "Crime Detection" club is energetic 12-year-old Nick Johnson (left), who is using a professional fingerprint kit on Dick DeGowin, a club member. Their parents are: Prof. and Mrs. Wendell A. Johnson and Prof. and Mrs. E. L. DeGowin. (Press-Citizen Photos.)

School Boys Hold Their Own Classes

Serious students of the techniques of crime detection are these three professors' sons. Left to right—Joe Howe, Clarence Updegraff and Howard Berg. Their parents are: Prof. and Mrs. J. W. Howe, Prof. and Mrs. C. M. Updegraff and Prof. and Mrs. C. P. Berg.

New York Conductor Will Be Soloist Here

Dimitri Mitropoulos, conductor of the New York Philharmonic orchestra, will be piano soloist tonight for the second successive year in a concert presented by the University of Iowa symphony orchestra. The conductor (above) awaits his cue in final rehearsal from James Dixon, 523 East Burlington street, who will conduct two selections. Mr. Dixon, formerly of Guthrie Center, came here to study on the advice of Mr. Mitropoulos, who took an interest in the student conductor's career four years ago. The concert will be at 8 p. m. in memorial union. (Press-Citizen Photo.)

Jim Dixon, Rolando (U-High Class of '52), and fellow student teacher, U-High, 1952

L to R: Author, Lou, John, Joe H., U-High, 1951.

Mary, Jean, Della, author, Tom K., Rod, Karen, Lou, Joe W., U-High 1951

L to R: 1st Row: Howard, Clare. 2nd row: Al, John. 3rd row: Joe W., author, Nick, Lou.

Rythmaires; 1st row: author, Joe W., Frank, Don, Nick. 2nd row: John R., Howard, Clare, John P. 3rd row: Lou, Al.

Author, Nick, Lou at U-High Mount Vernon Exchange Assembly, 7Nov1949

1203 Friendly Avenue, Chum II

1203 Friendly Avenue

Family photo for Christmas card, 1203 Friendly Avenue

Junior Counselors in kitchen, Camp Algonquian, Burt Lake, MI, 1950. Senior Counselor, (fifth from the left), Bill, was the older brother of Dr. Robert Kretzschmar on UI faculty.

Paving Here Nearing Completion

New concrete paving on North Lucas street between Iowa avenue and Jefferson street is rapidly nearing completion with one of the final sections being poured this afternoon. Final concrete is expected to be poured by the end of this week. (Press-Citizen Photo.)

Horrabin Construction Company, 1952

Prepare Bloomington, Lucas Streets for Paving

Excavation work on East Bloomington street between Governor street and Union place (above) this week marked the beginning of the paving program in Iowa City this summer. The paving in this block is expected to be completed in the latter part of next week. The William Horrabin Contracting Co., of Iowa City, is doing the paving.

IOWA

Second Parking Lot Being Paved

Paving is now underway on the second of the three municipal parking lots being paved this summer. Shown above is the Iowa avenue lot between Gilbert and Linn streets, where paving is now going on. Already completed is the paving on the South Dubuque street lot. The third lot, the College street lot, is now being prepared for paving. Total cost of paving the three lots is $32,674. The cost is to be paid from parking meter income. (Press-Citizen Photo.)

Site of strike for common labor wages.

Robert G. Carney, MD, 1215 Pickard Street.

Lt. Robert G. Carney, MD

Dotty Carney, Bobby & Patty at 1215 Pickard Street.

Reunion at Club. Photo courtesy of Don Blome.

Lady Ethel Whitby in Hampton Court Palace

The Neighborhood
(1935–1955)

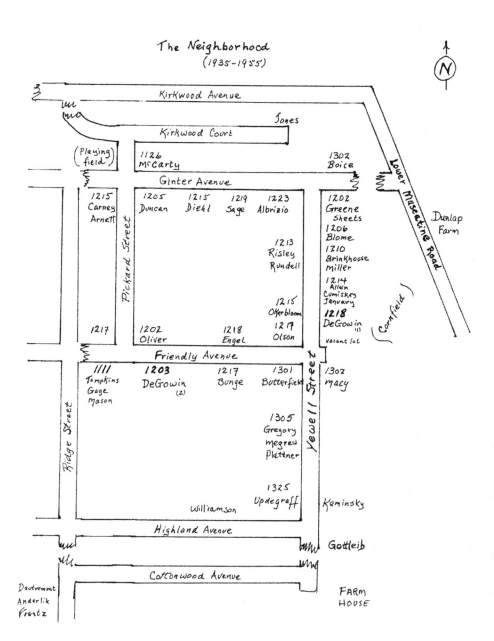

Chapter XI
Survival of the Free World in Doubt

Except for several US naval victories later in 1942, it was a bad year for the Free World. The Japanese Army had defeated Allied Ground Forces in the Pacific, and after the sneak attack on Pearl Harbor crippled the American Fleet, Japanese naval vessels, spotted off America's West Coast, seemed poised to invade California cities. After WWII, Admiral Yamamoto Isoroku was asked why his forces had not invaded the American homeland, to which he replied, "I would never invade the United States. There would be a gun behind every blade of grass."

Franklin Roosevelt, serving an unprecedented third term as president leading to a dictatorship, his critics alleged, issued Executive Order 9066 on 19FEB1942, imprisoning in concentration camps 120,000 men, women, and children of Japanese descent, many American Citizens, who had been living on the West Coast.

Adolf Hitler had conquered Europe and had begun "ethnic cleansing" of the Jewish population, confiscating their money and property, sending them to concentration camps to die from starvation, disease, or in gas chambers. Nazis killed over 6 million Jews during the holocaust, of which we knew little at the time. Firearms are the first private property confiscated by totalitarian governments. After Passover, on 19APR1942, 1,500 desperate Jewish men and women in the Warsaw Ghetto used the pistols, rifles, and shotguns they had hidden from the Nazi Gestapo to fight for their lives. For nearly a month they beat back the Wehrmacht, killing several hundred German soldiers before being overwhelmed, killed, or sent off to die in concentration camps.

A good democratic government rules by the will of a free people whose elected leaders trust their constituents to freely possess and use guns for self-defense, hunting, and the sport of target shooting. Indeed, the Supreme Court ruled, in The District of Columbia vs. Heller and in Chicago vs. McDonald, that the Second Amendment secures to the individual American Citizen the right to keep and bear arms, pursuant to the original intent of the Founders—Washington, Jefferson, and Mason. Early in WWII, Americans, who insist on such a right, shipped thousands of their personal firearms for home defense to British Citizens, who even then were restricted in their possession of guns.

At the beginning of 1942, we were losing the war. Our army was small and unprepared due to budget cuts, and still in the Great Depression, our economy vital to our defense, was in shambles. When, as an eight-year old child, I voiced my fears that a foreign army would soon invade American soil, or that Franklin Roosevelt who presided over wartime controls— former President Hoover agreed that "economic fascism" was necessary to win the war—might become a dictator like the enemy's axis leaders, Mother said, "You must have faith that these things will not happen, and America will prevail." Repeating her words assuaged my anxiety.

Service on the Home Front
Spared the devastation wrought by WWII in foreign cities, Americans united to support the war effort at home. Those of my relatives not in

uniform performed services essential to winning the war. For example, Mother's brother, Uncle George, served as council on Senator Harry S. Truman's Committee to assure the proper distribution of Foreign Aid to our allies. My father's brother, Uncle Milton, worked as an electrician in a defense plant in Portland, Oregon.

War department officials and medical school deans, recognizing the desperate need for army doctors, initiated the T-6 Program, a curriculum running year around that graduated physicians for the Armed Services in three years instead of four. My father, then 40 years old, was one of a total of 6 faculty members, now there are well over 200 members, in the Department of Internal Medicine responsible for teaching medical students the diagnosis and non-surgical treatment of disease. In addition to caring for patients, he continued his research on blood transfusion.

Moreover, as Secretary of the Subcommittee on Blood, Committee on Shock of the National Research Council, he traveled by train to Washington, D.C. once a month to attend the meetings of the Council. With Brigadier General Douglass Kendrick, Admiral Lloyd Newhouser and others, Elmer DeGowin developed the first blood transfusion program for the Armed Services. He wrote the Army handbook for establishing and operating a blood transfusion service.

My father was awarded a "B" gasoline rationing windshield sticker permitting him to buy enough gasoline to get him to work, he dropped me off at school on his way to the hospital, and I took the bus home. Government edicts restricted highway speed limits to 35 miles per hour to save gasoline. We missed those times of family outings, Sunday drives, and vacations were put on hold until the end of the war.

In the vacant lot next door on Yewell Street, we grew vegetables in our Victory Garden to eat fresh and for Mother to can. She baked bread and coped with books of ration stamps to purchase butter and meat, like food stamps, only she had to pay for them. She saved grease in tin cans for munitions manufacture, and flattened empty tin cans, turning them in to scrap metal drives for the war effort.

My friends and I collected newspapers, old tires, inner tubes, and scrap metal for Boy Scouts and other service organizations scrap drives. We pasted 10-cent saving stamps in a little booklet until they totaled $18.75, entitling us to redeem them for a $25 US War Savings Bond that matured in 10 years. I can't explain how $18.75 became a multiple of 10. Except for recycling, our consumer habits of the Great Depression prepared us for austerity during WWII.

Navy Neighbors

Across the street from the Field House, during a ceremony on 15APR1942, sailors raised the American Flag, and President Virgil Hancher turned over University of Iowa facilities to the US Navy. Next month, the first group of naval aviation cadets, 242 strong, arrived in Iowa City to begin their training at the Navy Pre-Flight School. Marching from the train in their sharp navy uniforms to the cadence of their own band, these young male athletes created quite a stir among the coeds and high school girls along the route to the South Quadrangle and Hillcrest dormitories, their homes for several weeks. This scene repeated, every two weeks for the next 3 ½ years, until 7DEC1945, infused Iowa City with an economic boom, including, it was rumored, the development of an "escort service" provided by non-student ladies of the community.

Future astronaut, Senator John Glenn, the first man to orbit the earth, went through the Pre-Flight program for his training in WWII. Cadet athletes from colleges around the country played on the Iowa Pre-Flight

School's football team, the Sea Hawks, beating teams of the University of Iowa in 1943 and 1944 by 25 points. Ironically, a cadet player from Michigan, Forest Evashevski, became the Hawkeye coach in the 1950's taking Iowa to Rose Bowl victories. My classmates, who lived on the west side of town near the school, introduced me to the obstacle course constructed for the cadets behind the football stadium where we swung from ropes across water and climbed obstructions when the cadets were occupied in classes.

As our former neighbors on Yewell Street left for the service or other teaching positions, Howard Moffitt rented his houses to naval officers, the faculty of the Pre-Flight School. Lieutenant F.S. "Red" Cumiskey, with wife Betty and dog Chum, rented and moved into the house next door to us at 1214 Yewell Street. In Risley's former home at 1213 Yewell Street, Commander Rundell and his family from San Angelo, Texas, joined our neighborhood. C.A. and John-Lee Rundell, with strange Texas accents, were about my age and joined in the activities seamlessly with the rest of us kids.

When Red Cumiskey was reassigned to duty in Indiana, Betty and he gave me Chum. She was part Collie and part German shepherd, resembling the latter breed. Chum was bright, beautiful, affectionate, and very protective. Red had taught her to heel without a leash, to "come" (in German), "sit, stay" and to fetch and carry the newspaper in her mouth for him. He wrote me from the flying field facilities at Purdue, where he trained naval cadets, asking about Chum and telling me of his work in Lafayette. I had the responsibility for feeding and grooming her, and Chum and I spent two wonderful years together walking and playing until she started over-protecting us from the new mailman and the paperboy. While I was quarantined with the mumps—an officer of the Johnson County Health Department had stapled next to our front door a cardboard sign proclaiming my affliction in letters legible from the street, restricting me to "house arrest," now a violation of patient privacy laws—my parents, sensitive to my strong attachment to my first dog, gave her to a kindly farmer who needed a watchdog. Chum was happy with the freedom to roam the fields, the farmer was happy, the mailman was happy, and the paperboy was happy, but I missed my loyal companion.

THE FARM

In the fall of 1941, Mr. Reagan subdivided his cornfield that stretched from our backyard on Yewell Street to his farm house four blocks to the east on Lower Muscatine Road. He auctioned the lots to potential home builders, but there was no threat of urban "sprawl," because the buyers could not obtain building materials during the war. So they planted Victory Gardens on their new properties, providing me with a view of Hugh Dunlap's small farm across Lower Muscatine Road from Mr. Reagan. Mr. Dunlap had returned from service in WWI to work as a building contractor in Iowa City. Then, during WWII, he was a Commander in the Navy's Seabees, building airfields in the Aleutian Islands to defend Alaska from invasion by the Japanese. Mrs. Dunlap, a nurse, and her four children, ran the farm while her husband was off to war.

Many days after school and on weekends found me walking east on Ginter Avenue's dirt extension from Yewell Street to the Dunlap farm to play with Jimmy, the youngest of the family, but a year or two older than I. After watching Douglass Fairbanks, Jr. swing from the rigging of a pirate ship to engage British sailors in swordplay in the Saturday afternoon movie matinee at the Englert Theater, Jim and I climbed to the haymow of his barn. There, in our imagination, we became pirates of the Spanish Main. Swinging from ropes hanging from rafters, we alighted on bales of hay, fencing with blunt dowels affixed with tin can hand guards—our

Spanish rapiers. Battles fought with wooden rifles in cornfield and pasture followed John Wayne's war movies.

His distinction as the youngest sibling gave us an abrupt reality check at 5:00 PM when his mother's, "Jimmeee!" echoed over the din of battle. Reluctantly, we ceased fire and headed for the barn where Jim had the chore of milking six cows, requiring his twice daily ministrations. Having little success starting a stream, when he gave me an opportunity, I was impressed with Jim's skill at bringing forth a jet of milk spattering into a stainless steel bucket or squirting into the mouth of the expectant cat, sitting by the wood milking stool, waiting patiently for a swallow of fresh warm milk. Jim pitched hay to feed the cows, slopped the hogs with sour whey and garbage, or shoveled manure out of the barn. I had failed to appreciate the hard dirty work required to take care of livestock from my First Grade's field trip to Mr. Dane's farm where we watched a hired man pick corn, slid down a haystack, and ate ice cream.

Of our many rural adventures, Pigeon hunting was one of our favorites. Farmers, living along Lower Muscatine Road, welcomed us to climb the rafters in their barns to catch the pigeons that roosted there, fouling with their excrement everything below. We kept some as pets and released others. The farmers were also pleased when we decimated the annoying flocks of sparrows with our bee-bee guns. When we were older and trusted to respect firearms, we spent hours punching holes in tin cans, plinking in the pasture with our .22 rifles. Before Jim was old enough to get a driver's license, he drove us around the pasture in the family's Model-A Ford pickup truck or on the tractor, a practice common for many farm kids in those days, I'm sure. After college and the armed service, Jim flew workers to oil rigs off the coast of Florida in a helicopter.

Chapter XII
Responsibility and Trust

In retrospect, my chores during my grade school years seem paltry compared to Jimmy's farm chores, but I had the responsibility of feeding and caring for "livestock," my pets. At one time or another they included my dog, Chum, a calico cat, a white rabbit, a guinea pig, a turtle, a chameleon, two Australian Zebra Finches, and a variety of pigeons. The rabbit had a recurrent scaling infection of his ears, requiring periodic treatment with a medicinal salve. I cleaned my room, carried out the garbage, and burned the trash.

Limited in activity by bouts of severe back pain from the inflammation of paraspinal ligaments and muscles, eased by using crutches or a cane, the result of an injury acquired during the heavy labor of summer jobs, my father willed to me his tasks of mowing the lawn, spading and weeding the garden, shoveling snow from the porch and driveway. My weekly allowance of 30 cents allowed me to join friends at a movie for 10 cents, buy popcorn for 5 cents, and blow the rest on candy at MacLachlan's grocery store, now gone, near the site of Lensing Funeral Home at 605 Kirkwood Avenue.

After training in the responsible care and handling of firearms, when I was 12 years old, my father gave me a single-shot .22 rifle, a Model 67-A

Winchester with blued barrel and beautiful walnut stock. I used it for target shooting and plinking, carefully cleaning and oiling the gun after each outing. As a result, it shows little wear today, stored, locked away in a safe place. I keep it as a symbol of my dad's trust in me. After WWII, my friends and I took war souvenir guns and our own shooters to show each other in high school. Michael Fody, one of our 9th grade student teachers, a veteran and a gun collector, brought some of his guns to our biology class to show us students and the other teachers. He invited several of us boys to his home in West Branch for lunch and to see his collection one weekend. He let me fire one of his flintlock pistols so that I would understand the state of technology in the American Colonies of the 18th Century.

No one ever thought of bringing a gun to school to shoot our classmates. Massacres of school children, college students, and military personnel never happened until the late 20th and early 21st Centuries. Charles Krauthammer points out in his column "Massacre at Newtown," published in the *Washington Post*, 20DEC2012, that "Every mass shooting has three elements: the killer, the weapon and the cultural climate." Of course one party and the mainstream media indict the weapon and would eliminate the problem if only there were no opposition by the other party to confiscating from over 100 million US citizens their 300 million firearms. Members of the opposing party point out the impossibility of doing that and what happens when you disarm the law-abiding public as the British liberals did when they first required registration of personal handguns, assuring gun-owners that they could keep their guns, and then confiscated them in 1998. Gun-related crime increased 40% by the year 2000. Scotland Yard reported that between September and November of 2001 robberies on the streets of London increased 100% from 8,614 in 2000 to 19,248 in 2001 (*The Press-Enterprise*, 4JAN2002). Not surprisingly, the BBC reported that residents of Birmingham, Manchester, and Nottingham were under increasing assault by armed criminals.

First Job

A man of inflexible habits, my father read the newspaper every morning before leaving for work and taking me to school. When the *Des Moines Register* began arriving only a few minutes before we left for work, Dad realized that our paperboy had quit. This job opening, in the spring of 1945, was temporarily filled by Mr. Griffith, the local circulation manager. Catching him delivering papers to our neighbors on our way to school one day, my father volunteered my services, and I promptly became the new carrier-salesman for the daily and Sunday issues of the *Des Moines Register*. Having just celebrated my eleventh birthday, I was elated by this sudden thrust into the business world of print journalism. I was gratified by Father's confidence in me and by his assurance that the experience would build a strong work ethic. It did not occur to me until later that now my dad would receive his paper to read before going to work.

Not neglecting to plan for my retirement 50+ years hence, I signed my Social Security Card, issued shortly after my eleventh birthday. To protect against identity theft, it lies, displaying the childish scrawl of my signature, in our safety deposit box. I've long since memorized my Social Security Number, because I had to write it every noon on a voucher to charge lunch in The University Hospitals Cafeteria. When my friend, Harold Shipton, challenged the cashier, stating that use of the Social Security Number for any purpose other than employment and retirement benefits violated federal law, she replied, "That is not your Social Security Number that we require you to write on the voucher. It is your University Number. They just have the same digits."

At the time, the *New York Times* was the only newspaper that had garnered more Pulitzer Prizes than the *Des Moines Register*. Many of the Register's prizes were awarded for Jay N. "Ding" Darling's political cartoons that graced its front page. The first Duck Stamp, Ding's work, celebrated its 80th anniversary in 2014. A great friend of conservationist President Herbert Hoover, Ding Darling established the wildlife refuge, named for him, on Sanibel Island, Florida.

I was proud of my work as a paperboy. It meant arising in the dark to the ringing of my wind-up Westclox Alarm Clock, before my parents awoke, retrieving, and counting my papers, folding them for throwing, then mounting my bicycle with papers in a canvas shoulder bag to deliver before 7:00 AM. I hit most porches with papers thrown from my bicycle as I rode on the sidewalk, but some customers required that I put the paper in the storm door. Friday after school and Saturday morning, I collected 35 cents from each customer, tearing a stamp-sized receipt, labeled with the week's date, from a stack of perforated cards bound at the top by two rings holding rectangular aluminum covers.

Most customers were a pleasure to meet and chat with each week, hearing their compliments and complaints. Several invited me into their modest homes to warm up on cold days, giving me edible treats on holidays. I found it difficult to deal with the few deadbeats who put me off from week-to-week, saying they had no cash right now. Their inability to come up with 35 cents left me to make up their deficit from my enormous $3.50 weekly profit. We never heard of a minimum wage.

Chapter XIII
Allied Victory

Nineteen forty-five brought sadness and joy. Before President Roosevelt could witness the end of WWII, he died on 12APR1945 of a cerebral hemorrhage in Warm Springs, Georgia, a resort for patients afflicted with sequelae of poliomyelitis. He was the only President I had known, "President Roosevelt," synonymous with the "President of the United States." The announcement that Vice President Harry S. Truman had succeeded FDR brought mixed reviews like, "He don't know beans," but it turned out that he did.

As General George S. Patton's victorious US Third Army fought valiantly through Germany under the Allied High Command of his former colleague and subordinate in the nascent tank corps, General Dwight D. Eisenhower, and as the Russian Army entered Berlin, Adolf Hitler shot himself. His mistress, Eva Braun, took cyanide in their bunker on 30APR1945. Admiral Doenitz surrendered Germany unconditionally on VE-Day (Victory in Europe), 8MAY1945, setting off celebrations across America.

Doggedly, the Japanese fought on, desperately flying Kamikaze suicide planes into the ships of Admiral Chester W. Nimitz's Pacific Fleet. Despite naval victories, and those of the army led by Eisenhower's former commander, General Douglass MacArthur, Japanese soldiers and civilians were determined to fight to last man on the Japanese mainland. My father-in-law, Master Sergeant Ernest A. Sivesind, was among those US troops preparing for the invasion of the Japanese homeland. Intelligence experts predicted casualties of one million American men and several million Japanese soldiers and civilians in the fighting. With these estimates in mind, President Truman authorized Iowa native, Colonel Paul W. Tibbets to drop an atomic bomb, "Fat Boy," from his B-29, Enola Gay (named for his mother) on the industrial city of Hiroshima. The atomic explosion vaporized much of Hiroshima on 6AUG1945, but the Japanese leaders refused to surrender until after the second bomb was dropped on Nagasaki on 9AUG1945.

Atomic detonations in both cities killed about 120,000 people outright and induced the Japanese to surrender on 14AUG1945, VJ-Day. General MacArthur, familiar with oriental culture, told Dr. Roger Egeberg, his doctor, that the supernatural aspect of the tremendous explosions permitted the Japanese leaders to "save face" and surrender, saving millions of lives. America's jubilation on VJ-Day, marking the end of a 6-year global conflict that killed an estimated 55 million people, surpassed that of VE-Day. The horror of the devastation caused by the atomic bombs ensured that a nuclear war was delayed, at least for the last 70 years.

With feelings of great relief and elation, we celebrated the end of the war and the end of gasoline rationing in September 1945 by taking a vacation. It was the first respite in four years of my father's seven-day work weeks. He was determined to visit his sister and her family in Traverse City, Michigan, where his father was living. Grandpa, at age 85, was glad to see us. It was the last time I saw him. He died the next year.

Orthodontia and the O.S.S.

"Are you DeGowin?"

"Yeth," I replied, mumbling through a mouthful of wires, ligatures, a suction tube, and cotton sponges.

"I roomed with your uncle in Cairo, Egypt," said this brisk man wearing an army officer's uniform.

He had caught my eye as he entered The University of Iowa Dental Clinic, six rows of dental chair stations to my right, with Dr. Higley, my orthodontist. With the end of WWII, my five-year battle with braces, oral surgery, and retainers would soon be over. Dr. Higley and his dental students had worked to straighten my teeth, for a total of $50. As the visitor admired their work, probing my teeth with his fingers, Dr. Higley introduced his guest as Captain Robert Moyers, DDS. He was returning to work with Dr. Higley on the Dental Faculty after serving with distinction in the European Theater of War. He would be my new orthodontist.

The O.S.S.

Later, Dr. Moyers told me that his former roommate, my Uncle Ed—who never discussed with me his service in the O.S.S. (Office of Strategic Service)—had recaptured from the Italians, the crown jewels of the King of Ethiopia, Hailie Salassie. He had returned them to the King to secure his loyalty in preparation for the Allied invasion of Italy during WWII.

"Wild Bill" Donovan, recipient of the Congressional Medal of Honor for heroism in WWI as Colonel of New York's famous Fighting 69th Regiment, accepted President Roosevelt's invitation to leave his successful law practice in Buffalo, New York, and develop during WWII, Roosevelt's personal intelligence gathering and special operations unit, the Office of Strategic Service (O.S.S.). As the wartime predecessor of the Central Intelligence Agency (C.I.A.), established by President Truman in 1948, O.S.S. agents engaged in clandestine operations behind enemy lines to destabilize the Axis war effort. They were popularly known as the cloak and dagger boys.

ROBERT MOYERS, DDS

His movements were quick, yet his speech betrayed a rural twang, so one's first impression of Dr. Moyers in mufti did not permit one to accurately speculate on his career. This short, wiry, clean shaven man with light brown hair and glasses had grown up in a small town in southwest Iowa. In addition to his work as an ordained Presbyterian Minister, he performed as a trick rider in rodeos. Employed as a carpenter to defray his college and dental school expenses at The University of Iowa, he had worked summers for Moffitt, helping to build our house at 1203 Friendly Avenue in 1941. He once showed me where he had worked on the mantle of our fireplace.

WARTIME SERVICE

After leaving Uncle Ed in Africa, Bobby Moyer's new assignment in the O.S.S. took him to fight the Nazis with guerrilla forces in the mountains of Greece. He told us that he parachuted into Greece at least 16 times, sometimes at night. He described several different ways to blow up German munitions trains. Although trained as a dentist, he served the Greek partisans as a medical officer, setting fractured arms and performing minor surgery. After WWII, with the issue in balance, the US State Department flew him back to Greece to persuade his former comrades-in-arms, who were communists, to support the new democratic government; he did and they did. The Greeks named in his honor, the Robert Moyers Memorial Hospital. He was knighted by the British Crown for his service in the Allied cause during WWII.

Dr. Moyers left the dental faculty at Iowa after a few years to become Professor and Head of Orthodontia at The University of Ontario Dental School in Toronto, Canada. In the spring of 1955, as I was completing my third year of premedical courses at The University of Michigan in Ann Arbor, my parents told me that Dr. Moyers had been recruited by Michigan to establish and direct The Institute for Human Growth and Development.

One day, while I was studying in the crowded Medical Library, I was surprised to spot my former orthodontist, Dr. Moyers, poring over a journal at a table by a window. It had been at least five years since I had seen him, but I thought surely I recognized him, so I went over and standing behind him, tapped him on the shoulder, not thinking that my appearance might have changed since I was 16 years old, now 21. Quickly, he turned around and glared at me puzzled, wondering, who was this over-familiar, impertinent student who had interrupted his study. I wondered if I had mistaken his identity when a smile of recognition crossed his face. Without wasting time on pleasantries, oblivious to students now looking in our direction, he stood up, turned me to the window, parted my lips with his fingers and examined my upper incisors to see how well his orthodontic work at Iowa had held up.

A year later, Jack Moyers, Bobby's brother, spoke at an orientation that I attended before beginning work as a Medical Nurse Assistant (an orderly) at the University of Iowa Hospitals in the summer of 1956. In contrast to Bobby's diminutive stature, Jack was taller and more robust. Later, when Jack was Professor and Head of the Department of Anesthesiology at University Hospital, he lived a half-block away from us on Dill Street in Iowa City. Thereafter, I was able to keep track of the activities of my former peripatetic orthodontist.

Chapter XIV
University High School 1946-1952

THE DEBATE

"Thwap-Thwap-Thwap-Thwap."

"What is that noise, Clare?"

"The snow is freezing on the expansion joints," Clare replied as he turned up the speed of the windshield wipers. It was snowing harder now, large sloppy clumps of snowflakes spattered on the windshield as we sped east at 75 miles per hour on US 6.

Earlier that afternoon, while summing up our closing arguments on the 1951 high school debate question, "Should the United States further extend the Welfare State?" we had seen through the classroom windows of Newton High School, that the somber gray skies of March 8th had darkened and had started releasing a few lazy large snowflakes.

Armed with small boxes of 3″x 5″ index cards filled with numbers and their attributions, we six U-High juniors had come to this state debate contest prepared to back our positions. Cards belonging to our affirmative team bore statistics supporting President Truman's contention that Americans could not afford to be without Federal Health Insurance, while cards of the team members on the negative side had statistics from the recent Hoover Commission Report showing how bureaucracies wasted tax money. The team predicted that "Fedi-Med" would be much too expensive, and intrude on the practice of medicine to the detriment of the patient and his or her doctor. How prophetic! Clare debated without cards in front of him. When I asked him how he remembered all of the statistics he used to support his argument, he said, "I don't have to remember them. I make them up."

Now, the snow was covering the plowed farm fields, turning the pitch black Iowa topsoil white. Ahead, a pickup truck entered the highway from a side road on our right and skidded 180 degrees to stop, facing the ditch in our lane. Only then did I realize how slick the road had become. Clare slowed to 70 miles per hour and passed the truck in the left lane. Although Iowa's speed limits specified driving at what is "reasonable and proper," driving 70-75 miles per hour on an icy road in a blinding snowstorm stretched a liberal interpretation to call it legal. For a moment, I wondered if I had been wise to ride in the back seat of Clare's 1948 Mercury Coupe, hurtling down a slippery highway at breakneck speed, instead of riding home with our mature and cautious debate teacher, Mr. Charles Balcer, in his new 1950 Ford Sedan. Wisdom had nothing to do with it. It was the thrill of speed that was decisive.

I admit that afternoon's 90-mile ride from Newton to Iowa City challenged my adolescent view of immortality, but we arrived safely before dark at school and waited for our classmates to arrive in our teacher's car. They didn't come, so we assumed that Mr. Balcer had taken our friends directly to their homes. It was only when Howard, who had ridden with our teacher, arrived at school the next day with fresh scratches on his forehead and on the bridge of his nose that we learned what had happened the day before. Mr. Balcer drove cautiously the whole way at 35 mph, reaching Coralville, only two miles from home, when suddenly his car started sliding on a patch of ice, slowly skidded off the road into the ditch and rolled over. Our faithful teacher sustained a broken wrist, and his passengers survived with scratches and bruises. Automobiles equipped with seat belts were years in the future. I am glad I survived my ride down US 6, because I cherish memories of good friends, excellent teachers, outstanding academics, and extracurricular activities at U-High.

ACADEMICS

If someone at our 50th Year U-High Class of 1952 Reunion asked me, "How did your high school prepare you for college and enrich your life?" I might have replied that my teachers showed me how to acquire, retain, analyze, and use information for work and pleasure, and how to communicate verbally and in writing.

ENGLISH

Rebuking us for talking while we struggled with one of his daily quizzes, our 7th Grade English Teacher, Dr. Millington Farwell Carpenter, stood in the back of the classroom, humming, when he wasn't scolding us, turning the crank of his ancient mimeograph machine that spewed out, "clickity-clack," fragrant copies of tomorrow's quiz or the responsive reading for the Friday Assembly. His quizzes, testing our knowledge of syntax, gave us the option of choosing the correct word in a sentence like this one, "On July 2, 1863, Lee's orders to assault the Union left flank at Little Round Top called for the troops of General A.P. Hill's XXX Corps, which was/were waiting on Seminary Ridge, to move forward in support." Dr. Haefner claimed in jest that Dr. Carpenter taught more Civil War history in English than he did in Social Studies.

It was hard for us to imagine that "Carp," as we called him among ourselves, now in late middle age, had been a track star and currently coached the upper class track team. We saw him as a portly bespectacled unkempt bachelor with a shock of uncombed white hair and bushy eyebrows. He worked in his shirtsleeves, his suit coat draped over the back of a chair. Wide suspenders held up his trousers over which his generous paunch protruded. It spread the bottom of his shirt front to reveal a navel that winked at us like a cyclopean eye with each turn of the crank of his mimeograph machine. Earlier that morning, his belly had captured, as a shelf, bits of breakfast that had missed his mouth, leaving stains of jelly, egg, and coffee on his shirt.

Carp had a deep booming voice capable of intimidating the most challenging student. One of his favorite epithets was, "Dumb as a Dyke." It referred to Peter Dyke, who with his twin brother, Jan, had joined our 7th Grade in the fall of 1946. They came from Puerto Rico, where they had been living and attending school before their father, a medical officer with US Army, had been assigned to Iowa's Department of Preventive Medicine. Carp's epithet was not only humiliating, ensuring instant discharge if uttered these days, but it lacked insight. Peter was fluent in Spanish, and spoke English with an accent, but he wasn't dumb. After two years Dr. Dyke was assigned elsewhere, and the twins left our class. I had not seen Peter for 15 years until I met him on the parade ground of Fort Sam Houston, San Antonio, Texas. Attending the Medical Field Service School as newly commissioned Captains in the US Army Medical Corps, we had just completed our residency training, his in Neurology at Yale University Medical School and mine in Internal Medicine at The University of Chicago. After discharge from the service, I recall seeing his name as author, writing in the medical literature as a member of the Yale faculty.

Dr. Carpenter, as we addressed him in class, started a trend for which I am grateful. Each week he required us to write a theme of two or three pages in length. He, or one of his student teachers, read and corrected each paper and assigned a grade. English teachers at U-High expressed the idea that we should learn to write by writing. That meant that I wrote a theme each week for six years in English courses from the 7th through the 12th grades. Our teachers contended that demanding students to memorize many rules of grammar and to spend hours diagraming sentences wasted time better used for writing. Quizzes were designed to help us use proper syntax by selecting words and sentence structure that "sounded right." It occurred to our lovable 12th Grade English Teacher, Dr. James Day, that unless he did something soon, his students might enter college asking, "What is a noun?" He saved us that humiliation by giving us a remedial crash course on nouns, verbs, adjectives, etc.

My father learned that members of the Admissions Committee paid special attention to a well written autobiographical sketch, required for the application to The University of Michigan, using it to evaluate applicants by the directors of freshman courses. So I worked hard on the sketch, editing and rewriting, and it paid off. While standing in Waterman Gym to register for the two semesters of English required of all entering freshmen at Michigan, I was identified, pulled out of line and assigned to an honors class taught by Dr. Arthur Carr, an associate professor. I enjoyed the class, which required writing a number of papers, and because of my experience at U-High, I garnered a grade sufficient to excuse me from the required second semester. With that reprieve, I elected a course on American Authors, letting me squeeze in more liberal arts courses within my 18 semester-hour premedical requirements. Thank you Drs. Carpenter, Day and all those other English teachers of grades 8-11 who made us write.

I hope to continue learning how to write. Swallowing pride, I greatly benefitted from colleagues, coauthors, and medical editors who critically reviewed my research paper and textbook writing before publishing. After I retired, my twelve classmates and teacher in the 2001 Iowa Summer

Writer's Festival Course on Memoirs gave especially valuable advice, a humbling experience for which I am grateful.

For the life of me, I could not understand the French spoken by the natives during a visit to Paris years ago. Surprisingly, however, I was able to translate French texts in the Parks Canada brochure and in the Visitor Center in Coteau-du-Lac, Quebec, more than a half century after taking French at U-High in grades 7th through 9th. Moreover, I found that I could translate priests' entries, written in French, in copies of church registries of baptisms, marriage contracts, and burials of my Irish and French-Canadian ancestors.

Dr. Helen Eddy served as U-High's first principal when its doors opened in 1916. Sometime before that, as a free and foot-loose teacher, Miss Eddy had spent at least one summer touring and studying in France. Now, nearing retirement, this graying proper lady interrupted her didactic approach to teaching eight of us how to read French, and, in reverie, a smile crossed her face as she described the French people and their beautiful countryside that she remembered so fondly.

Miss Eddy taught pronunciation, but it was only when Dr. Camile LeVois or Madame Pauline Aspel taught her class that we heard true Parisian French spoken. As 7th graders, we marveled at news' photos of the atomic test explosion at the Bikini atoll in 1946, but they were eclipsed by a photograph we saw later of the young well-endowed Madame Aspel, wearing a Bikini on a beach in Southern France. I had not seen her for 50 years until she read a poem she had written commemorating the opening of Iowa City's new Woolf Avenue Bridge in 1998. Speaking with her after the dedication reminded me of her charming French accent and joie de vivre. My friend, Joe, was so impressed with Dr. LeVois's advice, "If you want to learn to speak French, you should live in France," that after he retired, Joe and Susan spent six months each year living in the Burgundy region of rural France.

MATH

"Do not buy a textbook of geometry. We will write our own text in this class. First, we will define terms, and then we will develop theorems to describe relationships. Let's start with you and then go clockwise around the class. I want each of you to give me your definition of a point. Then we will define a line." If you think that is easy, try it.

With these words, Dr. H. Vernon Price broke the uncharacteristic silence of our loosely disciplined classes at U-High. None of us had uttered a word since entering the classroom for the first meeting of 11th grade geometry. Dr. Price sat upright at a desk in front of the blackboard, silently reading each of the 14 registration cards we had filled out. We saw a slender man of medium height in his early 40's. One might easily mistake him for a movie celebrity with his sharply defined facial features and carefully combed coal black hair. Immaculate in a spotless gray suit with vest, it could have been custom tailored to fit. He wasted no words or motions. His deliberate movements were precise whether writing definitions or drawing perfect geometrical configurations on the blackboard. His appearance and demeanor demanded our respect, and later our realization that he cared for his students, assured our affection.

Unlike my brilliant classmates, I struggled with math, lacking their intuition to conceptualize the steps between the start to the proof of problems that the authors of math textbooks invariably omitted. In spite of my handicap, completing U-High's math courses with passing grades exempted me from taking additional math courses to fulfill premedical requirements at the University of Michigan, so I took a course in logic, instead.

I cannot recall depending upon geometry or trigonometry in later life except for using the Pythagorean Theorem to calculate a hypotenuse of 75 feet to purchase line for each anchor to secure our houseboat on sandbars in the Upper Mississippi River.

While most of us elected to take Dr. Price's 12th Grade course in Trigonometry and Introduction to Calculus, Clare forsook his senior year in high school to enroll as a full-time freshman at Iowa, replete with a "Joe College" brush cut and a new baby-blue Buick convertible, a gift from his parents. Howard enrolled in a graduate math course in The University of Iowa. Graduate students taking the course must have been more humiliated than I had been by my classmate, because Howard, as a high school student, got the top grade in the course.

After graduating from U-High as our valedictorian, Howard attended on scholarship, The California Institute of Technology. He obtained his degree with Nobel Laureate, Linus Pauling, graduating at Cal Tech with a grade point of 4.33, on a 4-point scale. His A+ was the highest grade point recorded there in the previous 5 years. Following a Fulbright Fellowship at the Carlsberg Laboratories in Copenhagen, Howard entered Harvard Medical School. With an interest in bench research, he obtained a PhD in Experimental Physics instead of the MD. After teaching molecular biology at The University of Colorado, and later at his alma mater, Cal Tech, he returned to Harvard as Professor of Molecular Biology with a joint appointment at the Land Laboratory in Cambridge, Massachusetts.

READINGS IN SOCIAL STUDIES

Without hesitation, I rate Readings in Social Studies as the best course I took at U-High. It was taught by Dr. John H. Haefner, the best of many excellent teachers I encountered during 19 years of formal education. From his course, I developed a life-long desire to read non-fiction literature, especially history and biography. In the short term it was excellent preparation for college courses. In 1951 when I enrolled in his elective course as a senior, Dr. Haefner, a WWII navy veteran in his mid-thirties, was short, slender, fit, and quick in his movements; a good friend of Vernon Price. With his ready smile, he engaged his 15 students as co-investigators in a search for truth in the background of history. He taught by asking questions, the Socratic Method, which I, and many others, later employed teaching clinical medicine. Medical students today think the practice is humiliating, don't like it and call it "pimping."

Our first assignment taught us how to write answers to an essay test, a skill valuable to college students in the 1950's, when professors gave such tests, read the answers, and assigned a grade. Dr. Haefner gave us guidelines on how to determine what was asked, how to apportion time, and how to organize a coherent response. He gave essay tests, so we had lots of opportunities to practice what we had learned.

There was not one specific textbook for the course. The books Dr. Haefner assigned, published in hard cover in the Modern Library Series, sold for a bargain at $1.25 each. Because they were inexpensive, printed on cheap paper, he encouraged us to underline select passages and make marginal notes in pencil. Dr. Haefner led the discussion on those salient points underlined in pencil. His questions clarified the text and led to our consideration of the various aspects of philosophy and political science. I've saved all of my books, the pages of which are yellowing but legible after 60 years.

The assignment of each book saw us in the University Library to find out as much as we could about what was going on at the time and place the book was written. This meant reading about the Borgias and the Italian City States of the 16th Century during the discussion in class of Niccolo

Machiavelli's *The Prince* and the *Discourses*, a treatise describing statecraft, applicable to today's leaders.

Reading about the 5th Century B.C. Athenians and the Greek City States opened a new world for me as we looked into the background for Plato's *The Republic*. Recently, I've thought about Plato's assertion that we could achieve Utopia when "Philosophers are Kings." Substitute political ideologues for philosophers, and you have the totalitarian dictators of the 20th Century. To supplement our understanding of the Socratic Method, as depicted by Plato, each of us were tasked to paraphrase a Platonic Dialogue.

A Member of the local American Legion contacted Dr. Haefner, concerned that he was teaching communism in the state school during the witch-hunting period of the 1950's Cold War. We were reading US House Document #619, a Government Printing Office publication, *The Strategy and Tactics of World Communism*. Congresswoman Frances P. Bolton of Ohio had compiled, in this single source, copies of the works of Karl Marx, Lenin, Stalin, and other Soviet leaders. They claimed that Communism could only flourish by the overthrow of all democratic governments, and that any means, no matter how deceitful or violent, should be pursued to that end. Their assertion that once a Communist Dictatorship ruled the world, the State would "melt away" was ludicrous. Dr. Haefner contended that citizens educated in a democracy should read these tracts, because it would convince them of the perfidious nature of the advocates of communism, the fallacy of their arguments, and lead free people to reject them out of hand. He asked the Legion member, "If you don't know about communism, how can you combat it?"

Assigned as supplemental reading, George Orwell's *1984*, published in 1949, reinforced our notions about the evils of Russian Communism. He described a future in which government agents with surveillance cameras and wiretaps would monitor citizens' communications, speech, and behavior. How unlikely that would happen in America, we thought at the time. Yet, the revelations by Edward Snowden in 2013 about how the President of the United States has permitted his National Security Agency to spy on American Citizens by collecting data on their telephone communications, ignoring the protection of the Fourth Amendment, shows how prescient Orwell was.

Dr. Haefner reconvened Readings in Social Studies in a Conference Room at the University Hospitals at 4:00 PM Saturday afternoon, 12MAY1990. Premier Gorbashev had recently presided over the collapse of the Soviet Union. When he retired, Dr. Haefner returned Joe's Platonic Dialogue, retained for use in his university education classes. On its receipt, Joe called me from Phoenix to propose a reprise of our class.

Forty years after our revered teacher called our first class to order, 10 of our 15 classmates returned to class, including: John H. Haefner, Professor Emeritus of Education, U. of I.; Mary, Teacher at Metro School Cedar Rapids; Rolando, Opera Singer, Boston and Rome; Sarah, Docent, National Building Museum, Washington, D.C.; Leonard, Attorney, Winterset, IA; Joe, Judge, Phoenix, AZ; Nick, Professor of Law, U. of I.; Tom, Professor of Pathology, U. of I.; Lou, Professor & Chairman of Geology & Geophysics, U. of Wisconsin-Madison; Don, Engineer, Avionics Group, Rockwell Collins, Cedar Rapids; and me as host, Professor of Internal Medicine & Radiology, U. of I. Those absent: Rod, Pediatric Dentist, Denver, CO; Howard, Professor of Molecular Biology, Harvard; Steve, Rector, St. John's Episcopal Church, East Lyme, CT; John, Internist, Green Bay, WI; and Leo, Surgeon, Riverside, CA.

"If Mikhail Gorbashev walked through that door right now, what are the questions you would ask him?" Dr. Haefner asked us as he began the class in the same way he had led it in high school. The vigorous discussions of politics, foreign and domestic, that consumed the next hour revealed that my middle-aged classmates, who had completed 4 to 8 years of advanced education after high school, had retained the same political views they argued 40 years previously when they debated the merits and shortcomings of the Welfare State. So much for the value of a higher education; what a waste of tuition! In spite of such diverse opinions, the day was a very enjoyable occasion, concluding with a dinner honoring Dr. Haefner, and the presentation to him of a Waterford Crystal Apple, by his former students and their spouses.

Assemblies

All six (6-12) grades at U-High attended the school's assemblies, held in front of the stage in the gymnasium, where, with his hand over his heart, our Principal faced the American Flag and led us in the Pledge of Allegiance. There was no reference to "under God," added in 1954 by Congress to assert that America was not an atheist state like the Soviet Union. We remained standing to read in unison from Dr. Carpenter's mimeographed sheets, "WE hold these Truths to be self-evident, that all MEN are created equal, etc., etc." Thomas Jefferson, an inveterate slave master, was said to have had second thoughts after writing these words in the Declaration of Independence, but we had no such ambivalence about them. Without the benefit of "affirmative action" (a code word for racial profiling), we had no classmates of Jewish faith or with black skin at U-High. Discrimination was condemned by our parents and teachers, and there wasn't any, because we had no one to discriminate against. Some of us felt deprived, because our counterparts at City High were able to not discriminate against Kent, a friend and former classmate, who used to bring matzos and jelly to class during Passover, or against Paul and Larry. Helen Lemme Grade School in Iowa City is named for their late mother, a friend of my family and an active member of the NAACP.

Chapter XV
The Johnson County Bureau of Investigation

For the lone college student, whom we were shadowing, to be unaware of his two tails meant that he was lost in thought or didn't care why these silly kids were following him on Capitol Street in front of the Chemistry Building. He could hardly help from noticing Nick one-half block behind him or me on the other side of the street, because the street and sidewalks were devoid of other pedestrians and vehicles for three blocks in either direction. Testing the chapter entitled "Surveillance" in our handbook, *How to be a Detective*—ordered from an ad in the back of a comic book— we concluded that this technique would serve us better on the crowded streets of New York where we would be less conspicuous than on Iowa's deserted campus that Saturday afternoon.

Our field work followed the weekly Saturday morning meeting of our Detective Club at the home office, not at 221-B Baker Street, London, but in Nick's bedroom in his home on Melrose Court. There, five of us seventh grade boys—inspired by the exploits of Sir Arthur Conan Doyle's Sherlock Holmes—met to devour treatises on criminal law for the lay- man, to learn how to develop fingerprints with lamp black, to lift them with Scotch Tape, and to analyze them, counting loops and whorls. On one occasion, Nick, our Director, arranged with Chief of Police Oliver

(Ollie) White to take our fingerprints at the Police Station and submit them to the Federal Bureau of Investigation. The FBI reported back that they were unreadable. Later, Nick wrote Director, J. Edgar Hoover, offering our services as the Johnson County Bureau of Investigation to assist the FBI in the Iowa City area. Hoover, who took time out from chasing bank robbers, kidnappers and communists to reply, declined the offer, but he sent us several books about the FBI to supplement our study materials.

Nick's interest in detective work arose from visits to the office of Richard Holcomb, a former Chief of Police in Kansas. Professor Holcomb taught courses in the university and produced in the summer, the Peace Officers Short Course for Police Officers, Sheriffs and Officers of the Iowa Highway Patrol. With his encouragement, we registered and attended lectures and workshops on how to gather evidence at the crime scene, on mock trials, and on crowd control. We considered farfetched, in 1947, the scenario proposed by one lecturer in which he tasked his audience to prepare a tactical response to Iowa students staging a riot, but the riot came to pass 20 years later when mobs of students trashed storefronts in downtown Iowa City, protesting the Vietnam War. Nick recalled that we got the highest scores on the course final examination.

Shortly after a columnist for the *Iowa City Press-Citizen* wrote a human interest story about our Detective Club that featured a photograph of the five of us 12-year old kids, we disbanded. Well, our cover was blown. No longer could we shadow, incognito, suspicious college students and other questionable suspects. Whether this extracurricular activity bore fruit later in life, I cannot say. Howard's PhD was in experimental physics, and Clare and I were awarded the MD. However, it may have sparked an interest for Joe H. and Nick, who both obtained law degrees.

After graduating from The University of Arizona Law School, Joe practiced law in Arizona before leaving for Harvard Law School. He taught there and later attained an advanced law degree, LLM. Thereafter, he served on the Law Faculty at Western Reserve University and then as Visiting Professor of Law at The University of Iowa. Incredulous that his colleagues in academia teaching criminal law had not participated in actual court trials, he returned to the West to practice law in Phoenix. He was soon recognized as an attorney of competence and integrity by the Governor of Arizona, Bruce Babbitt, who appointed him a District Judge, Maricopa County (Phoenix).

Nick graduated from The University of Texas Law School. He then served as law clerk for Federal Circuit Judge Brown in Texas, and the next year, for US Supreme Court Justice Hugo Black. Completing his clerkship, he was appointed Associate Professor of Law, The University of California at Berkeley. A year or so later, he joined a prestigious law firm in Washington, D.C., whose most famous partner was none other than Dean G. Acheson, former Secretary of State in the Truman Administration. Shortly after the assassination of John Kennedy, President Lyndon Johnson appointed Nick, in 1964, Federal Maritime Administrator. He was 29 years old. The appointment conferred on him the rank of Rear Admiral in the US Merchant Marine and Commandant of the Merchant Marine Academy at King's Point, Long Island, New York. When asked during his Senate Confirmation Hearing if he had had shipping experience, he said he replied, "I once operated a canoe on the Iowa River, but not very successfully."

Later, President Johnson appointed Nick to a 7-year term on the Federal Communications Commission. Following his government service, Nick has taught law students as Adjunct Professor of Law at Iowa. With his commitment to improving education, he was elected to the Iowa City

School Board, and has served as a national advocate for better television programming, a critically needed effort. In 1972, twenty years after we graduated from high school, Nick gave the eulogy for the closing of The University Iowa Elementary School and the University High-School, taking university administrators to task for concluding that our alma mater was irrelevant. It was not irrelevant for us, and I hope it proved relevant for the student teachers, whom we joined in mutual education.

Physicians who make accurate diagnoses are able to prescribe therapy to relieve discomfort and, hopefully, return their patients to work and leisure, free of pain and anxiety. I do not know if my youthful aspiration to become a detective had anything to do with it, but I found exhilarating the process—eliciting clues from the patient's history (an eye-witness interview), extracting clues from the physical examination (observation of the crime scene), and integrating data from laboratory tests—enabling me to diagnose a here-to-fore obscure disease in a patient referred by his family physician.

Chapter XVI
The Music Man

A life-size statue, unveiled on 18MAY2002 at the entrance to The Music Man Square in his hometown of Mason City ("River City"), Iowa marked the 100th birthday of the late Meredith Willson. Invariably, the rousing strains of "76 Trombones" from the score of Willson's musical, *The Music Man*, bring to mind U-High's music man, not Professor Harold Hill of the musical, but Charles L. "Luke" Luckenbill, my first surrogate father.

After a two-year respite from an uninspired introduction to instrumental music, and with encouragement from my friend Lou, who had joined Mr. Luckenbill's rejuvenated school band as a budding tuba player, I was curious to see if band or I had changed now that I was a freshman (1948). Descending U-High's basement stairs, I turned right at the bottom and wended my way through workbenches toward the sound of a flute emanating from behind the door of the Band Room at the south end of the Shop. I looked in to see a pretty 8th grade girl, who later would become Lou's bride, playing the flute while her teacher sat next to her turning the pages of her lesson book on a music stand. Without looking up, he motioned me to enter and wait.

A new coat of cream-colored paint covered the old state's institutional green on the poured concrete walls of the Band Room. Light from windows, extending half-way over the top of an outside moat separating the parking lot from the west side of building, brightened the room. The conductor's platform, made of boards nailed to two-by-fours, sat in front of one of the concrete pillars that supported the concrete ceiling beams. Concentric semicircles of collapsible wooden chairs and black metal music stands faced the conductor's stand. Acoustics were not as bad as you might suspect.

Mr. Luckenbill praised the flautist's playing, assigned her next lesson, and turned to ask what I wanted. Delighted to hear that I played the clarinet, he quickly persuaded me to rejoin the world of performing arts. In addition to scheduling my first clarinet lesson, he said, "Band practice starts at 7:30 sharp every morning, and by the way, we are forming a dance band. Would you like to join us?" Boy! Would I!

In retrospect, most adults whom I admired as a teen-ager seemed taller and older than in reality. Luke was of medium build and six feet tall. He had black slightly curly hair and black eyebrows offsetting pleasant features that broke into an easy smile. His deep voice revealed a trace of Northern Missouri drawl. Like his colleagues, he wore a suit and tie. He rarely talked about his family, but I gathered he came from humble circumstances and had worked hard all of his life. Before coming to Iowa City he had taught school in Missouri. Brasses were his principal instruments, but he played woodwinds and strings. He also repaired them, working part time for Pearl West in his music store on Dubuque Street. Luke had enrolled in the School of Music at Iowa to obtain a Master's Degree. As a veteran, I think he had support from the GI Bill, but his salary from U-High paid the rent for married student housing, the half-barracks where he lived with wife, Betty and daughter, Janet.

We called him Mr. Luckenbill, but during rehearsals of the dance band, he was "Luke." He kidded us, listened to us, and respected our opinions. We respected him, and we responded to his enthusiasm for classical and popular music. Our parents recognized him as an outstanding teacher who had recruited their children to a vibrant instrumental music program. So after only two years, we were all sad to see him leave Iowa City after the award of his Master's Degree.

He left for his next job as head of instrumental music at Grinnell Iowa High School, but during summer "vacations," he gave lessons, worked in a drug store, and helped a heating contractor install furnaces. After several successful years at the high school, he was appointed Director of the Instrumental Music Program at Grinnell College. With the success of the Broadway musical and Hollywood movie, *The Music Man*, Luke arranged with his president for its composer, Iowa's native son, Meredith Willson, to receive an honorary degree from Grinnell College. At the last moment, Grinnell's President Howard Bowen, nixed the award, claiming Willson's national fame and many achievements fell short of deserving Grinnell's recognition. Embarrassed and infuriated by Bowen's double-cross, Luke resigned forthwith.

Later I learned that Luke had accepted a job as Assistant to the President of Lyon-Healy in Chicago. Lyon-Healy was a huge music store on Wabash Avenue that sold pianos, band and orchestra instruments, and sheet music. Luke, the only musician in the firm, introduced a marketing program that graded, as to their degree of difficulty, scores and sheet music for band and orchestra, a great benefit to band directors in selecting music appropriate to the skills of their music students. Luke, Betty, Janet, and now Debbie, moved to a lovely home in Glen Ellyn, Illinois, from which Luke commuted to work.

We had kept in touch exchanging Christmas cards, but I had not seen Luke for 10 years when, in 1963, he telephoned me requesting an appointment for a routine physical examination. Now, on the medical staff of The University of Chicago, I was 29 years old, the same age as Luke when I met him. My examination revealed that he was healthy but overweight with mild hypertension and slightly elevated blood cholesterol. I advised him to stop smoking and prescribed a diet to reduce weight, blood pressure, and cholesterol.

Our friendship renewed, Karen and I met Luke and Betty for enjoyable weekend dinners at restaurants in Chicago's western suburbs. Luke had quit smoking, but during those pleasant evenings, I could not bring myself to nag him about his unhealthy choices from the menu that violated my prescription. Visits to the Luckenbills' home in Glen Ellyn led me to realize that the qualities, which attracted me to Luke and Betty as a teenager, were those I admired in them now as an adult.

On New Year's morning, 1JAN1965, Betty's call awakened us in Decorah, Iowa, where we were visiting Karen's folks over the holidays. Through her tears, Betty said, "Luke has passed away, and I wanted you to know." He had come down with influenza after Christmas, and after several days of fever, cough and muscle pains, he developed chest pain, was hospitalized in Glen Ellyn where he died of a heart attack at age 45 years. I had long ago recovered from my minor teen-age rebellion from my father, but losing my surrogate father was devastating.

LUKE'S LEGACY

Luke left my classmates and me with four years of pleasure playing music and enjoying a lifetime of music appreciation. In U-High's concert band and orchestra, we performed three or more concerts a year and played at assemblies and other events.

James Dixon

As a student teacher, Jim Dixon played baritone in the back row when he wasn't conducting the band under Luke's supervision. Jim, 23, from Guthrie Center, Iowa, had become a protégé of Dimitri Metropoulos, former Director of the Minneapolis Symphony Orchestra. At Jim's invitation, Mr. Metropoulos visited The University of Iowa to teach students and conduct the University Symphony after he became Conductor of the New York Philharmonic. Jim prevailed upon him to address our high school band, assembled for his visit in U-High's Band Room at noon, 22JAN1952. His head was clean-shaven, and he was dressed in a dark blue suit, garnished with a light blue necktie and handkerchief. He wore dark blue suede shoes. Sitting second chair first clarinet, I was close enough to touch this great pianist and conductor as he spoke for a half-hour, encouraging us to work hard at learning and enjoying our craft. After graduating from Iowa, Jim Dixon became Assistant Conductor of the Chicago Symphony. He returned to Iowa as Director of the University Symphony Orchestra, earning a national reputation for performing difficult works of modern composers.

All-State Band

Joe (Sidney) W. deservedly sat first chair first clarinet in the U-High Band, but my playing in the audition at City High in the fall somehow convinced the judges to rank me several chairs ahead of him at All-State Band during my junior and senior years. The All-State Band and Orchestra performed their concerts, after several days of rehearsals, at the KRNT Theater in Des Moines every Thanksgiving Vacation.

The Little German Band

Luke started The Little German Band with members of our dance band. Clare and Howard played their cornets, John played his trombone, our bass player, Lou, played Tuba, Joe and I played clarinets, Al, our piano player, played baritone, and Nick played the bass drum. Luke played the Flugel Horn. We served as a pep band, playing for pep rallies, football and basketball games, and other events. Once we were invited to play on a "float" in the University Homecoming Parade in downtown Iowa City. We sat on boards fixed to the top of a farmer's corn wagon, which he pulled with his John Deere tractor. The cool night air of the October evening did not impair our playing as much as the fact that some of us had not memorized tunes, like *Herr Schmidt*, in the little booklets affixed to our instruments with clamps. To put a positive spin on it, we sounded great when our carriage halted momentarily under a street light, but Nick was able to carry on with our concert, beating his bass drum in light or darkness.

The Rhythmaires

One Saturday afternoon found the members of our new dance band in the Shop next to the Band Room sawing up light plywood boxes. Luke had persuaded McGovern Funeral Home to give us, instead of discarding them, the wooden crates used to ship caskets. We screwed hinged sides to a flat front, affixing a slanted music rack fitted with a night light to the inside of the front piece. Painted blue with a large script R on the front, our fancy music racks replaced the black steel stands we had borrowed for our rehearsals. A couple of years later, Bill Meardon, who directed the biggest and best dance band on the university campus, generously gave us his old Masonite music racks when he replaced them. We looked pretty professional behind our "new" legitimate band stands, and to enhance our image, some of us started smoking cigarettes to look "cool," like our role models. This was ten years before the Surgeon General said these "coffin nails" were bad for you, but we should have known better.

Luke ordered our "book" of popular standard pieces, arrangements that had become classics of the Swing Era. Most were suitable for dancing like: *String of Pearls, Sophisticated Lady, Embraceable You, Body and Soul, Satin Doll, Harlem Nocturn, One O'Clock Jump, St. Louis Blues, Muskat Ramble,* and *Stan Kenton's Opus in Pastels.* We played these pieces in the late 1940s and early 1950s, the last years of the Big Bands. Our bandstand icons were Benny Goodman, Louis Armstrong, Glen Miller, Count Basie, Artie Shaw, Duke Ellington, Ella Fitzgerald, Nat King Cole, and Stan Kenton. We saw some of these artists perform in the main ballroom of the Iowa Memorial Union during university dances and concerts of Jazz at the Philharmonic.

We had a great time playing together, especially when we played well, in the groove. At the time, most of us had no clue what the future held for us. None of us became professional musicians. First trumpet: Clare, MD-anesthesiologist, Davenport, IA; second trumpet: Howard, PhD-Professor of Molecular Biology and Physics, Harvard; trombone: John, MD-internist, Green Bay, WI; first clarinet/saxophone: Joe (Sid) W., PhD-Professor of Economics, Swarthmore College; tenor sax: Don, PhD-engineer, Rockwell Collins, Cedar Rapids, IA; clarinet/baritone sax: Joe H., LLM-Judge, Phoenix; drums: Nick, JD-Professor of Law, U. of Iowa; bass: Lou, PhD-Professor and Head Geology & Geosciences, U. of Wisconsin-Madison; and piano: Al, MBA-Vice President for Corporate Affairs, Miller Brewing Company, Milwaukee, WI. I played clarinet and saxophone. Luke asked me to manage the band, called the Rhythmaires. I scheduled our rehearsals, booked our gigs (engagements), and negotiated our fees. We played for dances at U-High, for high schools outside Iowa City, for Country Clubs, for an American Legion Club, for a street dance in Mount Vernon, Iowa, and for a rehearsal of a university musical production. We played for 3 or 4 hours at a dance and received $7.00 each, considerably less than union scale.

Al, our piano player with outstanding musical talent, composed the score for our ultimate performance, our senior play at graduation, *Genuine George*, (the phrase "real George!" was popular among teenagers at the time). I saved a copy of the script, describing a class reunion 20 years hence when space travel would be taken for granted, but only 17 years later Neil Armstrong walked on the moon.

Chapter XVII

50th Year Reunion of U-High Class of 1952

Karen and I arrived at North Hall, the uninspired new name of my former school building. A glance quickly dispelled my conviction that I would be the only member of the 32 of our 40 living classmates returning for our 50th Year U-High Class Reunion who looked old and overweight. Shortly after 5:00 PM, Saturday, 20JUL2002, our hostess, the Director of Social Work, escorted us through her department's facilities, housed in the former classrooms of the University Elementary and University High School where many of us had spent 13 years together in Kindergarten and grades 1-12. As small as they seemed now, those classrooms, the gym, the Shop and the Band Room brought back fond memories, long ago put aside.

Later, at a dinner in the State Room of the Iowa Memorial Union, the warmth of feelings for old friends and their spouses exceeded Iowa's 90+ degree heat and humidity of the evening. Dr. John Haefner's greeting and best wishes projected from a video-tape, made up in a small way for the absence of our revered teacher. Reminiscences, good-natured kidding, and good humor prevailed among friends, some of whom had known each other for 65 years and had not seen each other for 50 years. On Sunday, we met for a sumptuous champagne brunch in Shelter 3 of the Iowa City Park, which gave us another four hours to remember the things we forgot to ask or had no time to tell each other the previous day. We expressed our thanks to Del, Mary, Nick, John, and their spouses for organizing a wonderfully enjoyable reunion.

Half the 46 members of the Colossal Class of 1952 were from Iowa City and half were from neighboring farms and small towns like Coralville and North Liberty. Those from rural Johnson County townships had no high schools, so they attended U-High, the state school. Unlike members of some classes, we got along well with each other no matter where we called home. Nick's desktop publication of our class members' biographical sketches recorded the achievements of an extraordinary group of persons. Of the 42 classmates for whom we had data, 15 members pursued successful careers without obtaining academic degrees beyond high school, but many took college or business school courses after graduation. The highest degrees earned by others included: 10 BA, 1 MA, 1 MS, 1 RN, 1 MDiv, 2 JD, 1 LLM, 4 PhD, 1 DDS, 5 MD.

Three classmates became full-time farmers, and 6 started their own businesses. Four were homemakers, and two worked for the Federal Government. There were 3 professional musicians: an opera singer, a bassoonist, and a bandleader who made violins in his retirement. There was a hospital administrator, and 2 police officers, one of whom was Assistant Chief of Police of Iowa City. There were 2 lawyers and one judge. Of the 9 teachers, 4 taught in secondary schools, and 5 were university professors. One classmate was an Episcopalian Minister and Rector of his church. There was one nurse (who became a supervisor), a speech pathologist, a pediatric dentist, and 5 physician specialists: 1 anesthesiologist, 2 internists, 1 pathologist, and 1 surgeon. Their achievements are a tribute to their teachers, to their parents, to their own initiative, and to the opportunities available to them growing up in Iowa and in America.

INDEPENDENCE

Sre-e-e-ch! Gary "burned rubber" as he bolted away from me at a stop sign, accelerating east on Melrose Avenue in his 1948 Studebaker, leaving me in a cloud of dust. He had no fear of being arrested by police for drag racing, because he knew that law enforcement for University Heights was otherwise occupied at the moment; his mother was at home in the kitchen baking cookies. On duty as Town Marshall, his mom, Esther, cut a large formidable presence, dressed in her motorcyclist's black cap, white leather jacket, pants, gloves, boots, and sun glasses, seated astride her imposing black Harley-Davidson (Harley Hog) motorcycle. Portia, her phlegmatic loyal bloodhound, accompanied her when investigations called for patrol on foot. Gary showed me a steel tire-iron, he stowed under his front seat, anticipating a chance confrontation with an unwary motorist who might rear-end him when he stopped suddenly. After high school, Gary became a prison guard at Anamosa Reformatory.

MY FIRST AUTOMOBILE

Walking south on the sidewalk of Clinton Street between Iowa Book & Supply at the corner of Iowa Avenue to Whetstone's Drug Store on the corner at Washington Street, one could observe the grills of automobiles angle parked to the curb. All were American-made, none of Japanese or German manufacture, many of prewar vintage, each easily identified by make, model, and year by boys 14 years old with driver's licenses and aspirations for their own set of wheels to guarantee them independence from buses, bicycles, and parents.

It stretched credibility to call my first car a "hot rod." Father, concerned about the influence of movies like *Rebel Without a Cause*, which depicted actor James Dean drag racing and playing "chicken," permitted me to commit my savings from earnings on the paper route and other jobs to purchase a black 1938 Plymouth 4-door sedan for $275. This dependable means of transportation with little streamlining had conveyed, for 55,000 miles in the last 10 years, its elderly owner to the grocery store and to church on Sunday. Floor mats and mohair seat upholstery were only slightly worn. A gear shift with a black rubber knob arose on a rod from a hump on the floor between the driver and passenger requiring the simultaneous use of the clutch to shift gears. Despite its sluggish style, this old dowager opened a vast world of independence from bus schedules and parental restraint. It served me well for several years.

Seeking modern styling, I traded my Plymouth for a 1939 Oldsmobile Coupe, unaware of a problem, the previous owner (a mechanic) failed to mention. Nineteen thirty-nine was the year General Motors introduced the gear shift on the steering wheel shaft, and they had not worked out all the bugs. Unpredictably, when I released my foot from the accelerator, the gear shift lever jumped from third gear to neutral. It happened frequently enough so that in anticipation of suddenly losing forward drive, I drove holding the gearshift down with my right hand. I grudgingly accepted this inconvenience, because the cost to repair it exceeded my resources. This experience ensured that I employed an independent mechanic to check out used cars in the future.

Camp, 1950

On 25JUN1950, troops in the army of Communist North Korea, supported by the communist dictatorships of China and the Soviet Union, crossed the 38th Parallel to invade democratic South Korea. President Harry S. Truman, responding to critics who alleged that his previous inaction had lost China to the communists, ordered US troops, commanded by General Douglas MacArthur to protect the South Koreans and resist the invasion. This shocking news, broadcast on radios around the camp where I was working, concerned us 16-year-old junior counselors. Would we soon be called to service in another war? But the first to be called up were the veterans of WWII, now members of the Army Inactive Reserve, instead of those in the Active Reserve. Karen's stepfather, a Master Sergeant with 3 years' service in the South Pacific, was sent to Fort Lewis Washington, but soon he was discharged because of the legitimate protest by citizens who claimed these veterans had served their country in combat, and now it was time for someone else to report for duty. This so-called "police action," later called the "forgotten war," occurring only 5 years after the end of WWII, resulted in 39,000 casualties of United States and United Nations troops.

Working that summer at Camp Algonquian, eight of us roomed in a cabin near the rifle range. Camp Algonquian boys' camp was located on Burt Lake, a beautiful deep clear lake 8 miles long and 4 miles wide, surrounded by conifers and sandy beaches in Northern Michigan. As junior counselors we assisted senior counselors, many were University of Michigan football players, teaching campers how to canoe, sail, ride horseback, in the safe handling of firearms, and target shooting with .22 rifles. To defray expenses, we worked as kitchen staff, serving over 140 hungry campers and counselors with food prepared by Jim, a retired lumberjack cook, on his magnificent cast iron wood-burning stove and oven. During "free" time we were deployed to help Jonesy with maintenance work. He was the camp's carpenter and handyman, a strong wiry man of medium height in his early 70's, who could repair and maintain anything.

My favorite activities were horseback riding and target shooting. Colonel was my favorite horse. A "US" brand on his flank attested to his status as a veteran cavalry mount. Army buyers purchased horses for the cavalry when they were four years old. The US Cavalry dismounted to become mechanized and airborne in 1943, the horses sold to the public, so Colonel was about 12 years old when I rode this charger. His gait was smooth and sure, and he turned in response to neck reining without tugging on his bit. During a simulated Pony Express Race, he carried me at gallop to one end of a field, stood patiently for me to unsaddle and saddle him and then gallop back to the finish line ahead of the other riders.

We left camp on a pack trip early one morning as the sun was rising and the dew still on the grass beside the trail. We stopped after a few hours to give the campers rest and have breakfast, but my only memory of that was puckering up after drinking warm unsweetened canned grapefruit juice out of a tin mess cup. A more pleasant taste sensation was drinking my first bottle of cold beer sitting in front of our warm campfire after we tucked the campers in for the night.

Chapter XVIII
1203 Friendly Avenue
1946-1955

My parents reached middle age at the end of World War II, and with that milestone, they made two decisions: 1) they liked Iowa City and The University of Iowa and decided to stay long enough to 2) buy their first house. So in 1946, when father was 45, Mother was 46 and I was 12 years old, we moved but one block west from the house they had rented for eleven years from Howard Moffitt at 1218 Yewell Street to our new home at 1203 Friendly Avenue.

Friendly Avenue continued west for several blocks, intersecting at one point, with Lucas Street. We had friendly neighbors, but the significance of these street names escaped me until I learned that our street was named for Friendly Lucas, the Quaker spouse of Robert Lucas, who was appointed in 1838 as the first Governor of the new Territory of Iowa. Iowa City historian, Irving Weber, noted that Ginter Avenue, running parallel a block to the north of Friendly, was named for Larry Ginter, a favorite race horse owned by Robert Lucas, the Governor's son, who sold Moffitt the lots on which he built his houses in our neighborhood.

If I knew, I forgot how much the house cost, but real estate on the east side of town was considerably cheaper than on the west side where most of my classmates lived. None of them lived in a Moffitt house. Built in 1941 by Howard Moffitt, our house on Friendly was one of the last houses he built in Iowa City, and it was unique. The rounded front of the living room, capped by a conical shingled roof faced the street. A stone veneer siding enclosed the first floor, shingles the second. When I entered the living room from the front door on the west, I saw a stone fireplace to the left on the west wall and two sets of windows on the rounded north wall. Walls were plastered and cream colored. A door in the dining alcove on the east wall opened south to the kitchen from which I could enter the one-car garage on the left or descend the basement stairs through a door to the right. Initially, the house was heated with granulated coal fed into the furnace by a worm gear from a red metal bin, later replaced by a natural gas burning furnace.

If I had turned right into a hall running south after entering the front door, I would have encountered a narrow stairway to upstairs bedrooms, a clothes closet and a full bathroom on the left. Father occupied a bedroom across from the bathroom as his study. It accommodated his Smith Corona Portable Typewriter on a metal stand and his large gray Steelcase Office Desk, where he wrote research papers and his book.

To the right, off the upstairs landing, there was a small bathroom built into a dormer across from my parents' bedroom. An adolescent growth spurt caused me to duck as I entered the bathroom to shave peach fuzz from my chin. A door opened to left of the upstairs landing to my room. It was large enough for a single bed, a chest of drawers and a small desk. My north windows straddled the conical roof over the living room. As a child, unworried about finding plumbers, repairmen or heating contractors, or paying taxes or insurance premiums, I thought owning our own house was special.

Our new Moffitt house on Friendly Avenue was cozy but modest compared to the commodious homes where some of my high school classmates lived in Manville Heights on the west side of town, but I had not far to go for evidence that luxury is relative. Visiting friends Bill and Bob, fellow *Des Moines Register* carrier-salesmen, who lived 1 ½ blocks south on Ridge Street, soon convinced me of my good fortune. They lived with their father, mother, and younger sister in a small 3-room house, a former farmstead on the edge of Iowa City, which was later annexed. Their father walked ½ mile to catch the downtown bus to the Post Office where he worked; he had no automobile.

All that remained of the farmstead was the house, an old barn, and a vegetable garden on a small lot. Neighbors next door to the south had indoor plumbing, but my friends used a privy in the backyard. A hand pump at the kitchen sink provided well water for drinking and cooking, and another hand pump in the backyard conducted well water through a galvanized iron pipe, attached to the spout, then through a window to fill the wringer-washing machine in the basement. Sitting in the kitchen-dining room-living room with Bill one afternoon, I heard several "thumps" on the floor beneath my feet. When I asked him about it, he explained that corks hitting the basement ceiling made the "thumps" as they were ejected from his father's bottles of home brew fermenting beneath us on the basement floor.

TRUST

One day in the fall of 1945, the mailman brought my father a heavy cardboard cylinder (a 155 mm howitzer case), sealed securely by layers of dirty adhesive tape. Inside we discovered a disassembled 8 mm M1898 Mauser carbine, a WWII bolt action rifle of the German Infantry. Dr. Robert Johnson, an American Army Medical Officer, had "liberated" three rifles from a captured German guard house after the Battle of the Bulge to send them as souvenir gifts to his former teachers in Iowa.

Another recipient, Dr. Emory Warner, later Chairman of the Department of Pathology, assembled the rifle for my father, who gave the rifle to me. Of course, I would not shoot this high powered German rifle, but the next year, Dad presented me with a boy's rifle for target shooting. I've saved it, cleaning it after use to preserve its original luster after these many years.

Carl Gilles, MD, Professor of Radiology, accepted the third Mauser from Dr. Johnson. Red Gilles, was a fine gentleman, excellent teacher, and expert radiologist. Under his white coat, he wore a suit with vest, replete with a gold watch chain. As one of his students recalled, "He was a man comfortable in his own skin." His enthusiasm for his Civil War muskets was infectious as he generously shared with me anecdotes about the pieces in his collection. However, he told me that he stopped collecting antique firearms after WWII when he had to pay more than $5.00 for a specimen. Thereafter, he collected and repaired antique pocket watches and clocks.

"Work cures three Evils: Poverty, Vice and Boredom."
–Voltaire

In addition to delivering the *Des Moines Register* every morning seven days a week from 1945 to 1948 and the *Daily Iowan* from 1948 to 1950 six days a week, I worked at jobs in Iowa City every summer except for one summer during college, when I was in summer school. Paperboys delivered papers for modest pay, never for minimum wage, never for enough money to support a family, never for more than an introduction for young boys and girls to learn how to interact with customers, while at the same time, learning the value of money. Cousin Bob and I were amazed that his brother-in-law, a high school teacher in the Washington, D.C., area, could afford to spend three months' vacation every summer at Bob's family home in Northern Michigan where Jim spent the time riding his motorcycle and playing accordion for pleasure in a local bar. Neither Bob, an attorney, nor I could remember taking a vacation of more than three weeks from the time we were kids until we retired.

FOOD SERVICE

During the summer of 1948, Nick and I worked about 5 hours a day at $0.40 per hour for the noon and evening meals at the University Iowa Hospitals Cafeterias for employees, nurses, and doctors. With long-handled aluminum spoons and spatulas, I served food from large pans on a steam table to employees holding stainless steel navy surplus trays, divided into sections to prevent gravy from the mashed potatoes from flowing into the cherry cobbler desert. Rural Iowans ate dinner, their big meal, at noon. A state subsidy ensured that a low-paid hospital employee's dinner of roast beef, mashed potatoes and gravy, green beans, salad, a roll, peach cobbler, and coffee or ice tea never exceeded $0.37 at the cash register.

Nick and I learned a lot from our customers, other Nutrition Department employees, and college students, working for their meals. Some diners scolded us for serving miserly helpings of food, while others asserted that the same sized portions were too generous, but most smiled, chatted, and thanked us for doing our job. Displaying their personalities, whether hungry or not, gave us a reality lesson in psychology. From two deaf employees, we learned to "sign" the alphabet, a skill I retained to the surprise and gratification of several hearing-impaired patients I cared for years later. Another Nutrition Department employee, Polly, a plump woman with large lips, breasts and hips, that strained her starched white uniform, asked me, a naïve kid, "Do you like fruit?" When I answered, "Yes," she said, "Take a bite out of my ass. It's a peach!"

EDEN MOTORS

Despite my determination to outlast my predecessors, my job at the Kaiser-Fraiser Automobile Dealership, Eden Motors, on Riverside Drive, lasted only 4 weeks in May of 1951. Clarence Eden, the owner, always needed a car-wash boy and janitor, because high school students holding that job could stand his verbal abuse for only 2-3 weeks before they quit. I soon discovered that this avuncular man had the personality of a pregnant mink. Eden had earned a reputation as a demanding boss and hard-nosed businessman. Earlier, the *Iowa City Press-Citizen* reported that a customer had brought charges against him, claiming Eden had, following a heated discussion, ejected the plaintiff from his office by kicking him in the pants.

Although I worked hard for $0.75 per hour, washing and vacuuming cars in 20 minutes, sweeping out the showroom and hauling the trash to the dump, my work was never good enough to please Mr. Eden.

Two incidents convinced me to move on. First, none of the entire workforce worked Saturday afternoons. When I requested the time off, Eden said, "We will just have to find someone who will work then." Fat chance; he hadn't yet. Next a pleasant black man applied for a job washing cars, telling Eden he had worked in a 3-minute car wash in Chicago. After a test in which all of the mechanics told me they had timed the man, who had taken 25 minutes to wash a car, Eden, who hadn't watched him, claimed he had taken but 10 minutes. Realizing that I could never please or respect this liar, I resigned and fortunately have never worked for anyone like Eden since.

Johnson County Engineer

My high school friend, Steve, helped me get a job on the surveying crew for the Johnson County Engineer in June of 1951. After the disappointing experience pushing a broom and washing cars for Eden, my new job was a breath of fresh air, literally. Moreover, my wages increased 20% to $0.90 per hour.

On my first day of work, I met the Survey Crew: Bill Hetrick (foreman), Caesar Savedra (engineer), John, (labor), and two high school friends, Steve and Tom E.. Six of us piled into the county's van, and we headed for the dirt roads of rural Johnson County. I learned how to carry the "chain," a long steel measuring tape and hold the "rod" at the roadside so Caesar could sight through the telescope of his transit and read the numbers on the rod. From his readings, he calculated the elevations required for excavation or fill. At his direction, Steve, Tom, and I pounded numbered flat wood stakes into dirt on the roadsides to direct the graders who would later level the road and shoulders.

Except for the first day's second degree sunburn, which healed in a week, working hard outside on the dirt roads with a congenial crew at good wages, made up for the dreary beginning of the summer at Eden Motors. We worked well as a team, kidded each other, but treated each other with respect and good humor. I saw delightful scenery and chatted with friendly farmers on back roads whom I never would have encountered otherwise. It was a great summer job!

WILLIAM HORRABIN CONSTRUCTION COMPANY

Lying supine on the grass in the shade, I gazed up at the bottom of the truck when two anxious questions came to mind. Would I be able to pick up my shovel when the one o'clock whistle blew, and if I was able to return to work, could I survive until the whistle blew at 5:00 PM? Fortunately, the involuntary complete prostration of the noon hour rejuvenated exhausted muscles and lifted a flagging determination to finish the first day's work without collapse.

Jim, a life-long friend and classmate, and I graduated from University High School in May 1952. Searching for work, we considered maintenance jobs at high wages with Williams Pipeline Company of Coralville, working at their plant in Chicago, until we discovered that we would be scabs during a strike there by union members. Somehow, we learned that Horrabin had received a contract from Iowa City to pave the apron in front of the airport and streets in town. As one of the best paying jobs in town, Mr. Horrrabin was hiring common labor at $1.50 per hour. We found out later that contractors in Davenport, Iowa, were paying union labor twice that amount, but labor in Iowa City was abundant and cheap with many high school and college students looking for summer work.

My job was to pull, with Jim on the other side of the 8″ high steel forms, a recalcitrant 4″ x 16″ heavy wood beam across wet concrete dumped between the forms by a ready-mix cement truck. A compressor activated a vibrator attached to the center of the beam, which knocked down the concrete between the forms but transmitted coarse vibration to the iron wheels at the ends of the beam that rode on the forms. Attached to the wheels on each side, was a galvanized iron pipe ending in a "T"-shaped handle, which vibrated in turn as I grasped it to pull, with my coworker, this crude device over the fresh concrete, preparing it for the puddlers and the cement finishers.

When I awoke every morning that first week of work, I found that it took five minutes before I could fully open my hands or completely close them to make a fist. After two weeks' work, however, muscles in hands, arms, back, and legs finally stopped aching, becoming harder and stronger. It was fortunate recovery occurred when it did, because on our third Monday of work, Jim and I looked up from shoveling concrete to see two large muscular applicants for our positions. They were inquiring of our foreman, Fred Laughlin, if he was hiring common labor for our project at the airport. Fred glanced over at Jim and me to see two 18-year old high school graduates shoveling concrete as fast as they could. Fred turned back to the two Iowa football players and shaking his head "no," assured that Jim and I had acquired yet another incentive to give Horrabin Construction Company a good day's work every day that summer.

By the end of the summer, I realized the benefits of hard manual labor working at a job—we are told by immigration reformers—that US Citizens will not take. It felt good to have honest employment with reasonable compensation, to end the day with minimal fatigue, hard muscles and sound sleep, and to note that callouses on my hands had grown so thick that I could snuff out a cigarette in my palm without wincing.

Paul, who had graduated from City High in 1952, joined us as the only black person on our paving crew. Unlike me, he worked without a shirt, but after a couple of days in the hot sun, I was surprised to note that his back sunburned and peeled. He excelled without the benefit of affirmative action, non-existent then, earning a degree in physics at The University of Iowa. After graduation, he started his own successful software company in a south Chicago suburb and later served at a post in Washington, D.C.

Another City High alumnus joined us while we were paving the airport entrance road. Enlisting in the Army after high school, Bob served as one of General MacArthur's Elite Guard in Tokyo, all members of which exceeded 6 feet in height. Bob was 6′6″ tall, weighed 240 pounds, then an architecture student at Iowa State College in Ames. One night after work, Bob suggested that we check out the performance of his 1951 Ford, in which he had replaced distributor points and sparkplugs. At 105 mph on the recently paved Highway 1 south of town, I experienced a sensation approaching zero gravity, flying around some of the well-engineered curves. We were lucky the road was deserted and that we never illuminated in our headlights an Amish horse and buggy on the way home to Kalona.

If an upper arm deserved the tattoo, "Born to Lose," popular with convicts who fail to subscribe to the last lines of the poem *Invictus* by William Ernest Henley:

"I am master of my fate:
I am captain of my soul,"

it was George. He was in his 40s, scrawny, of medium height and incessantly whining about his troubles from which he could never seem to extricate himself. Paving streets in Iowa City during that summer of 1952, I was chagrined to witness a couple of other workers tease this poor soul. While digging ditches for storm sewer tile, his tormentors, assured they were unobserved by Fred, our foreman, approached George from behind in the ditch, let out a piercing whistle and goosed him with the long handle of a ditching shovel. Shouting "Y-e-e-o-w!," George dropped his shovel, jumped out of the ditch, and massaged his slightly traumatized posterior while trying to recover his dignity. The rest of us never knew when and if this would happen again, but it did, despite our pleas to leave the poor guy alone. After repeated assaults led to Pavlovian conditioning, his bullies needed only to step behind him and whistle for George to respond by yelling, "Y-e-e-o-w!," and quickly jump out of the ditch.

At the end of the week, George usually drank his Friday paycheck at the Oasis Bar on College Street. Attempting to drive home after closing one night, he encountered and sheared off a telephone pole, leading to his incarceration, a fine, and suspension of his driver's license. On that occasion, as on others, his brother bailed him out of jail. During another weekend binge, George awoke from a drunken stupor in Phoenix, Arizona, wondering how he had ended up 1,200 miles from home with no money. Through the haze, he vaguely remembered that during the previous evening, he had proposed marriage to the lady sitting on the bar stool next to him at the Oasis, but he couldn't recall what happened after that.

Chapter XX

Go West

Flashing headlights and roaring engines wakened us abruptly from our first few minutes of welcome sleep on the porch of an abandoned clubhouse. Three unwelcome pickup trucks circled us, drivers gunning their engines, then sped away. Threatened by we knew not what, we threw our bedrolls into our cars and bolted for town. Believing the City Square in downtown Chamberlain, South Dakota, was safe, we spread our bedrolls under trees and tried to sleep. Dawn's light revealed we had bedded down next to the City Jail. Maybe its proximity had discouraged further pursuit by our tormentors.

Six of us U-High graduates had worked hard that summer of 1952 and had decided to spend some of our earnings on a two-week camping trip before leaving for college or harvesting crops in September. Lou and Don rode with Joe H. in his 1948 Pontiac while Al and I rode with Gaylyn in his 1950 Bel Air Chevrolet. Both cars were comfortable, but neither had air conditioning. Without the benefit of light-weight tents, down-filled sleeping bags, or air mattresses sold at Cabela's these days, we coped with blanket-rolls, sleeping on rubberized sheets over hard ground or pine boughs under a canvas tarpaulin draped over clothesline rope tied to a couple of trees, our makeshift tent.

We found that the campground we planned to stay in at Chamberlain our first night out was coated in mud from a spring flood of the Missouri River, leading us to seek, what turned out to be only temporary refuge, on the porch of an abandoned clubhouse on a rural golf course. Passing through the sweltering Bad Lands introduced us to refreshing cool breezes, while sleeping on pine needles, in the beautiful Black Hills. A short stop near Devil's Tower at a village of prairie dogs to watch their antics, delayed us only slightly before climbing Boot Hill to find the graves of Wild Bill Hickock and Calamity Jane overlooking the town of Deadwood, South Dakota.

YELLOWSTONE

The clear blue water of Lake Yellowstone, shimmering in the afternoon sun, greeted us as we reached our westernmost destination, Yellowstone National Park. After negotiating a couple of "bear jams," traffic jams of tourists' cars stopped by bears soliciting handouts of marshmallows, we found an empty campsite at Old Faithful Campground. We tied up our tarpaulin, cooked dinner on our Coleman Stove, and joined, for beer and cheer, our former classmates at Old Faithful Lodge where they had been working that summer: Mary H., Mary V., Jean, Gretchen, Rod, and Tom E.

During the next several days, we explored the 180-mile circuit around the Park, noting the contrast of Iowa's lush rolling hills of corn and soybeans to this volcanic plateau with it steam geysers, steaming sulfur springs, bubbling mud pots, conifer-covered mountains, and the Grand Canyon of the Yellowstone River. At a gas station at the northern extremity of the park, Mammoth Hot Springs, Joe vowed that he would be pumping gas there at $0.36 cents a gallon next summer instead of at Bob & Henry's in Iowa City at $0.18 cents a gallon. He did and later found his bride working one summer in the park, a school teacher from Nebraska.

The Grand Tetons

A freezing rain followed by light snow during the night accelerated our departure from Yellowstone Park on Labor Day, 1SEP1952. Cold damp bedding precluded sleep, so at 4:30 AM we gave up, threw our wet blankets into the cars, folded and stowed with cold numbed fingers our ice-covered tarpaulin and headed out the south exit of the park for the Grand Tetons. On our way, the sun came out, dispelling the gray cold gloom as we entered the Jackson Hole region. From our campsite that afternoon and evening, we looked across beautiful Jenny Lake to see the sun and shadows play on the majestic snow-capped mountains beyond, wondering how many tourists translated the French, Grand Tetons, to English; "Big Tits."

Rocky Mountain National Park

Winter's onset in the mountains paused as we crossed Wyoming in a day to visit Estes Park and Allen's Park in Colorado's Rocky Mountain National Park. En route, gazing across the brown flat land, disturbed only by blowing tumbleweed and dust devils, we guessed how awesome the Rocky Mountains must have appeared to early western travelers. Ascending heights approaching 12,000 feet while driving up Trail Ridge Road, the scenery and altitude left us breathless as we walked to viewing points. One of us recalled the exclamation of Theodore Roosevelt when he first saw the spectacular snow-capped mountains, clear mountain lakes, and deep wooded canyons and declared its, "description bankrupts the English Language."

With another reunion, we located classmate Tom K., who had been working that summer, as an assistant for Dr. Posey (a hydraulic engineering professor from Iowa), on an especially constructed slough in a clear fast running mountain stream, Long's Peak rising in the background. Tom had finished the summer's project as we arrived that afternoon. Light held long enough for Lou to pan for gold in the mountain stream, but his lack of success in striking rich that afternoon failed to deter him from pursuing a stellar career in academic geology.

A vacant, old, small house on Dr. Posey's property provided a roof over our heads and a smooth dry floor on which to spread our bedrolls after an evening of celebration. "Clop, clop, clop" on the front porch wakened seven bleary-eyed celebrants at first light. A ghostly white apparition peered at us through the porch window as we struggled to regain our senses. Its bony-skeletal-like face, sporting a white goatee, finally made sense after we made out large pointed ears and horns on this curious domestic Billy Goat looking for breakfast.

Tom joined us for the 800+ mile trip home to Iowa City. Without the benefit of the Interstate Highway System, yet to be inaugurated by the Eisenhower Administration, we spelled each other, driving straight through in 16 hours. Driving across the vast open spaces of Colorado and Kansas, I mused with optimism and a little anxiety about what lay ahead in college, a time of transition from adolescence to adulthood, somewhat delayed for those of us pursuing more formal education, but immediate for Gaylyn, who would be farming for the rest of his working life.

Chapter XXI
The University of Michigan
1952-1955

"Hail to the Victors Valiant! Hail to the Conquering Heroes! Hail! Hail to Michigan!, the Champions of the West," rang out voices from Michigan Alumni and other guests, standing behind my mother, accompanying them on our upright piano in the living room of our home at 1203 Friendly Avenue in Iowa City. Responding to requests, she selected popular songs from sheet music stored in the compartment under the hinged lid of the piano seat. As a child and teenager, my parents included me in these informal dinners in which they entertained medical residents and their wives, the men, returning as World War II veterans, older and more mature than those in training before the war. Father's "perfect Manhattans" enhanced the singing, fellowship, and stimulating conversation at Mother's dinners. Many of those guests became life-long friends, in later years telling me how much they appreciated my folks' hospitality that provided a respite from their work in the hospital.

By the time I was a senior in high school, I could sing the Victors and other Michigan classics without reference to the score. Reminiscences of my parents' good times during their 10+ years in Ann Arbor, my visits there to the home of Aunt Frances and Uncle Rob, and its national reputation, enhanced my desire to attend The University of Michigan, the alma mater of my parents, aunts, uncles, and cousins. So when my folks said they thought that they could send me to college at Michigan, I jumped at the opportunity.

Many of my classmates planned to attend The University of Iowa, but though I would miss them, I viewed leaving home as a chance to make new friends from other places and to take advantage of an opportunity to become my own person, not the son of my parents, who were well known in the close academic community of small town Iowa City. Moreover, Father and I engaged in frequent, sometimes fiery debates, unwittingly fueled by my alleging that he should speak less dogmatically, a ploy I used after reading Wendell Johnson's *People in Quandries*, promoting the use of "scientific speech" of the General Semanticist. Incredibly, my father steamed but held his temper, though my arrogance must have infuriated him. Our separation with my departure was good for both of us.

So, on a day in mid-September 1952, after riding on a train all day, I walked south along State Street from the railway terminal to South Quadrangle, wondering what lay ahead. My parents scrimped to pay the $400 per semester out-of-state tuition, plus dormitory fees to send me to their alma mater, and I contributed as much as I could from earnings at summer jobs. Recognized nationally for excellence in academics and sports, Michigan accepted the top 10% of the state's high school graduates, claiming the rest could go to Michigan State College in East Lansing. New Yorkers flocked to The University of Michigan, because its out-of-state tuition was cheaper than Columbia University's and other private colleges in the East. I wondered if I could compete successfully with these bright fast-talking students from Michigan and New York.

Scott House of South Quadrangle

"Malcolm will be your roommate," said the Resident Head for the 7th floor of Scott House in South Quadrangle as he showed me to our room, my home away from home for the next three years. The newest residence hall on Michigan's campus, South Quadrangle had opened the previous year, home for 1100 students, divided into units of 175 men each in what was called the Michigan House Plan.

Shortly after surveying our room, bright, simply furnished for serious study, Malcolm entered the room, shook my hand, and started hanging up his clothes, talking as we got acquainted. He looked older than freshmen I had joined for orientation the day before, lean, muscular, several inches shorter than I, he was attending Michigan on the G.I. Bill with full disability payments as a Korean War veteran. Assigned to combat after entering the Army out of high school in Detroit two years previously, he had injured his back carrying 155 mm howitzer shells to an artillery battery. A healed scar from spinal surgery confirmed the story, but did not explain a linear scar on his left biceps. When I asked if it was from a battle injury, slightly embarrassed, he said, "No. It was from the surgical excision of a tattoo, obtained when I was drunk, of a former girlfriend's name."

Courses

Unsure whether I wanted to become a doctor, since I did not want to do it just to please my father, I enrolled in premedical courses, assured that though heavy on science, they provided a broad background for majors other than medicine. So in the first semester of my freshman year, I enrolled in 18 credit hours of courses in the College of Literature, Science and the Arts: Inorganic Chemistry, Zoology, Latin, English, History of Western Civilization, and World Political Geography. The latter course was the academic part of Air Force ROTC, which I elected instead of Physical Education.

This course load kept me studying every evening after supper from 6:00 to 10:00 PM weeknights. In addition to the excitement of learning new things in college-level classes, there were other incentives to study. My folks had sacrificed to send me away to school, competition for grades among premed students was stiff, poor grades meant no admission to medical school, or worse, losing a college deferment from the draft. Michigan kept distractions to a minimum: freshman were not allowed to have cars on campus, imbibing alcohol was prohibited in resident halls and until age 21, women students had hours for curfew, there were no mixed gender residence halls. Not surprisingly, there were no reports of binge drinking or sexual assaults on campus.

The objective information derived from Chemistry and Zoology appealed to me, but I enjoyed Professor Carr's honors course in English. Impressed by the cordial relations of Scott House's white Resident Head and his black roommate, I proposed, in my final English course essay exam, that racial discrimination could be abolished if white and black college students would room together and that the Armed Forces should fully integrate, as authorized by President Truman. I especially liked Professor Dunham's History of Western Civilization and elected his The French Revolution and Napolean.

No one was more surprised than I to learn that I didn't flunk out my first semester at The University of Michigan. Instead, I racked up a grade point of 3.78/4.00. It was a "B" in Latin, a course that I took, mistakenly believing that it would help me master the vocabulary of medicine, which denied me a "straight-A" average. Well, that first semester was the best of the six I spent in Ann Arbor. I discovered that there was more to college than attending class, studying, eating, and sleeping.

Saturdays in the Fall

On football Saturdays, our group from Scott House joined 106,000 fans in the "Big House" to watch Coach Benny Oosterban's Wolverines play an unspectacular winning football season. Even though they beat Ohio State in the last game of the year, shouts of "Boot Benny" and "Oust Ooster" resounded from fans, disappointed that the Maize and Blue would forgo a trip to the Rose Bowl.

Music

Student bands, they sounded professional, played swing and jazz for dances at the Michigan Union every Friday night. My dates wore dresses or blue wool skirts, angora sweaters, bobby sox, and two-toned saddle shoes. My attire, the "uniform de jour," was a button-down oxford cloth shirt, blue striped silk rep tie, gray flannel wool slacks, dirty white buck shoes, and a navy blue blazer.

The Choral Union Series in the magnificent Hill Auditorium featured performances by symphony orchestras, the Michigan Glee Club, pianists Rubenstein and Horowitz, Stan Kenton's Band, the Four Freshmen, and actors like Charles Boyer and Sir Cecil Hardwick in George Bernard Shaw's *Don Juan in Hell*.

Unlike students in Iowa City, actors' dialogues in films shown in campus town movie theaters were punctuated by cheers for the hero and hisses for the villain from the student audience, which felt compelled to participate in the show.

Campus Visitors

Prince Akahito of Japan, heir to Herohito's throne, was dwarfed by his host President Harlan Hatcher's six-foot plus stature as the two walked before a large crowd gathered on the Diag in front of the University Library.

Malcolm nudged me and whispered, "If you want to get your picture in the paper, go up to that little guy with Hatcher, and punch him in the nose."

Another visitor, playwright alumnus Arthur Miller, Pulitzer Prize winner in 1949 for *Death of a Salesman* and ex-husband of Marilyn Monroe, had attended Michigan in the 1930's when it was popular for students and faculty to espouse Communist doctrine. Quoted in the local newspaper, Miller lamented the apathy of the student body of the 1950's, but my classmates were studying to stay in school and retain their deferments from the draft. Moreover, by then they knew of the millions of Russians Joe Stalin had killed during the purges he undertook to consolidate power in the 1920's and 1930's.

President Eisenhower

Malcolm woke me with a voice filled with despair late on the night of 4NOV1952. Dwight D. Eisenhower had just been elected 34th President of the United States, spelling disaster, in the minds of Malcolm and his Democrat friends. They worried that losing the White House and Congress to the Republicans for the first time in 20 years would lead to the dismembering of the New Deal socialist programs. Of course, it was not only Republicans who created the landslide, but a clear majority of the electorate, tired of bureaucratic intrusion into their lives, disappointed with a foreign policy that failed to stop the expansion of Soviet hegemony, and shocked by the scandals of the previous administrations. Indeed, 34 million voters made their choice at the ballot box. Eisenhower's 442 electoral votes beat decisively the 89 electoral votes of Illinois Governor Adlai E. Stevenson.

Critics, liberal historians of Eisenhower, said his was a "do nothing administration." Yet, he kept a campaign promise, traveled to Korea and ended the fighting. He maintained world peace through military strength, derided by critics as "brinksmanship," preventing further encroachment on democracies by the Soviet Union during the Cold War. During the first year in office, he desegregated Washington, D.C., an act neglected by all previous presidents since the end of Reconstruction. Before the Civil Rights Movement, he overcame the resistance of Arkansas Democrat Governor Orval Faubus, deploying men of the 101st Airborne to ensure admission of black students to Little Rock High School on 25SEP1957. His domestic policy created jobs in a surging economy by facilitating transportation, developing the Interstate Highway System, and opening the Saint Lawrence Seaway to foreign shipping and trade.

SUNDAY LETTERS

Every Sunday, Father sat down at his Smith-Corona portable typewriter to "hunt and peck," typing a letter to me that arrived midweek. An essay on a subject of his interest followed the first few lines of greeting and remarks about the weather in Iowa City. Sometimes, I received a play-by-play description of an Iowa football game, coached the day before by Michigan's former star blocking back for Tommy Harmon, Forest Evashevski. Father knew him, admired him for returning Iowa to greatness on the gridiron, and called him Evy, like everyone else in Iowa City did. My dad reminisced about his days in Ann Arbor, commented on my courses and encouraged me. He usually concluded with remarks about the fall colors and Mother's and his health.

I appreciated his thoughtful advice and encouragement, and I usually penned a reply each weekend telling him about school and Ann Arbor. Our correspondence reestablished a bond with my dad, diminished between my ages of 15 and 18 years. Father continued writing his Sunday Letters throughout my three years in Ann Arbor and thirteen years in Chicago. I have saved most of these letters from my kind mentor and treasure them, rereading them with emotion now that he is no longer with us. Written before the era of e-mail and cheap long distance telephone rates, they are a rare testimony of my father's thoughts and beliefs, which I hope his grandsons will enjoy reading. How can our current way of communicating leave such a record?

Returning home to Iowa City for Christmas Vacation was a lark. It was good to be with my folks and to see my friends who had stayed in town to go to The University of Iowa. Our conversations confirmed that my decision to attend college in Ann Arbor was the right thing to do. I planned to spend time studying for final examinations in January, but the resolve was weak and time passed rapidly while partying with friends. Spring Break in March found me in Ann Arbor for the week, not with classmates cavorting on the beaches at Fort Lauderdale, Florida. I could not in good conscience ask my parents to fund a week in the sun when they had sacrificed some of their pleasures to send me to college.

SUMMER 1953

Thomas Hickey of Keokuk, Iowa, underbid Horrabin Construction Company to receive the contract for paving streets, sidewalks, and parking lots for Iowa City during the summer of 1953. Accompanying other college students who applied for work to pay for their education, I joined the Union to receive union scale of $1.75 per hour for common labor. To make a profit with his low bid, Hickey built his own concrete plant on the circus grounds in south Iowa City so that he would not need to patronize Horrabin's Ready-Mix cement trucks. Unloading 98-pound sacks of cement for the plant from a railroad car with a coworker convinced me that I must have been in pretty good shape.

After Hickey's dump trucks had disgorged their load of liquid concrete, it was my job as one of the "puddlers" to push with my shovel the mixture

194

of cement, crushed rock, sand and water—water content was critical for pushing—so that the mixture flowed to fill the lane between the steel forms, filling crevices, air pockets and remaining tight against the forms. As the summer wore on, Hickey concluded that he was losing money paying the cement finishers excessive overtime wages after 5:00 PM. The wet concrete was not setting up fast enough, so he put less water in the mixture by mid-afternoon. So at about 3:00 PM, the hottest time of day, the loads of concrete slid out of the dump trucks to form mountains of viscous goo. Instead of pushing it to flow into the forms, we had to lift this heavy viscous mass with our shovels, backbreaking work with temperatures in the 90 to 100 degree range. Though exhausted, somehow I persevered and kept my job.

One day when we were paving the parking lot north of the old Post Office, where Tower Place now stands, picket signs appeared suddenly on the job. All of us were required to join the Union to work for Hickey, but the Union Steward had decided that he wouldn't inform us students of the strike. Hickey's contract with the Union called for him to raise the wages of all workers halfway through the summer's job. But Hickey only raised the wages of the high paid cement finishers, not those of the common labor. Some of my non-student coworkers had families to support and pressing medical expenses. Hickey had broken his word. Energized by this injustice, I stomped over to the Union Boss, surprising him by demanding that he give me a picket sign. The other student workers, regarding their work as temporary employment, failed to join me on the picket line. After a day or so of the strike, Hickey relented and raised the wages for common labor a dime to $1.85 per hour.

Chapter XXII
Upperclassman

Duane, my neighbor in Scott House, South Quadrangle, a Mormon and a teetotaler, invited me to consider joining his fraternity. His fraternity brothers in the ATO House were friendly and welcoming, the house was in good shape, and the thought appealed to me. Fraternity brothers probably develop stronger lasting friendships than independents do, but after thinking about it, I realized how much I valued control of my time for study and leisure, so I declined to become a Greek.

In the fall of 1953, Malcolm moved in with Gordon. Cowan, from down the hall, moved in as my roommate. Cowan was from Toledo, Ohio. He majored in Chemical Engineering and attended Michigan on a Naval ROTC scholarship. He sang as a member of the famous Michigan Glee Club. Uniforms for both organizations had it all over my Air Force Blues, which critics said could be confused with those worn by Greyhound Bus Drivers. Cowan wore a black tuxedo with tails and white gloves for the Glee Club, and a navy blue officer's uniform with white hat for Naval ROTC drill. Premedical course requirements continued to dominate my schedule of 18 credit hours each semester for Chemistry, Physics, Zoology, Botany, and Air Force ROTC.

The anticommunist paranoia of Wisconsin's Senator Joseph McCarthy, longtime friend of the Joseph Kennedy family, spread to the Michigan Legislature. State Senator, Kit Clardy's committee held hearings in Detroit, calling several of our teachers to testify to their loyalty. My excellent Professor of Embryology, Clement Markert, had enrolled in the Abraham Lincoln Brigade to fight with the communist faction against the fascist, Francisco Franco, in the Spanish Civil War of 1936-1939, and he was alleged to have retained sympathy for the communist cause. As a result of the Clardy Committee hearings, Michigan lost Markert to Johns Hopkins where he accepted a professorship. Professor Mark Nickerson, a nationally recognized pharmacologist, left Michigan for a post in a Canadian university following the hearings. Professor Chandler in Mathematics also found more hospitable academic employment elsewhere.

Documentation declassified by the American and Russian governments in recent years confirmed the presence of a large well-organized Communist spy ring that had infiltrated academic institutions and government agencies in the United States during the Cold War. I doubt if our teachers were guilty of spying. They were never prosecuted. However, there is credible declassified evidence that Alger Hiss was a Russian spy (Shelton, C.: *Alger Hiss: Why He Chose Treason*, Simon & Schuster, Inc., New York, pp.330, 2012.) As a high ranking US State Department Official, he accompanied President Roosevelt, who was ill and dying, to the Yalta Conference which gave Joseph Stalin most of Eastern Europe after WWII. Moreover, Hiss, a Harvard graduate and darling of the left, is credited with writing the United Nations Charter, giving Russia veto power in the Security Council, rendering the UN impotent as an agent for world peace.

CHARIVARIA

Charivari or shivaree is a noisy mock wedding serenade in which friends of the bride and groom celebrate their nuptials with a cacophonic outpouring of racket from horns, banging on pots and pans, tin cans tied to the rear bumper of the couple's auto, etc.

Seven of us students, led by an English major, Al Smallman, selected Charivaria as the name of our group committed to the critique of contemporary fiction and poetry. We met once a week in the canteen in the basement of the Michigan Union to drink coffee and talk. Works of popular authors underwent our scathing reviews, like J.D. Salinger's *Catcher in the Rye*, and T.S. Elliott's *Old Possum's Book of Practical Cats*, the inspiration for the musical *Cats*. Ernest Hemingway's *The Old Man and the Sea*, published in 1952, led to his Nobel Prize in literature on 28OCT1954, but no prize from us. We thought *The Old Man and the Sea* was good, but not up to the quality of *For Whom the Bell Tolls*, *The Nick Adams Stories* and his other earlier work, our opinions duly recorded in the mimeographed pages of our publication, *Charivaria*.

Moo U

In 1954, students at Michigan gave vent in song to their chauvinism when Michigan State College of Agriculture and Applied Science in East Lansing became Michigan State University. To the tune of *Home on the Range*, they sang, "Moo, Moo, MSU, where seldom is heard an intelligent word, and the cows roam the campus all day," until Biggie Munn's Michigan State football teams started beating the Wolverines in Ann Arbor.

Summer School 1954

As long as I lived at 1203 Friendly Avenue during high school and college, I had summer jobs but during the summer of 1954, when I took a chemistry course to fulfill a premedical requirement, I retained my household chores including mowing the lawn. But then I did not have the expense of board and room.

Sweating through eight weeks of Organic Chemistry during the summer of 1954 was a challenge. Taking the premedical course at Iowa—designed to weed out prospective medical students—permitted me to concentrate on one hard subject and complete requirements for admission to medical school in three years. Dr. Hines gave two lectures back-to-back from 8:00 until 10:00 every morning five days a week in the amphitheater of the Chemistry Building, without the benefit of air conditioning. An examination every four days assured that we followed his advice to memorize the structural formulae and the reactions of organic compounds in hours outside the class, including while reposing on the toilet.

Every afternoon from 1:00 to 5:00 we attended a steamy laboratory brewing foul smelling compounds, justifying the students' name for Organic Chemistry as "goo & gunk chemistry." They called Biochemistry "garbage chemistry." Somehow, I got eight credit hours of a "B" grade in Organic Chemistry at Iowa, which transferred to The University of Michigan and permitted me to stay in the premedical program.

THE UNIVERSITY OF MICHIGAN 1954-1955

With the truce signed at Panmunjom on 27JUL1953, President Eisenhower ended the shooting in Korea and saved South Korea from a Communist takeover by North Korea and China. But the atmosphere along the 38th Parallel in the Demilitarized Zone (DMZ) was so tense that the military draft remained in effect. Father said, "Get as much education as you can before entering the Army, because your professional training will make the service to your country more valuable. Mr. Coder, head of the Johnson County Draft Board said, "Because of the University's location in Iowa City, we have many student deferments in this college town. This limits the number of eligible draftees to fill our quota, so I advise you to enter medical school after three years of college if you wish to continue your education on a student deferment."

Congressmen and others believed that drafting college students would eventually deplete the country of educated leaders. Even though medical students were not drafted, I knew that I would serve in the armed services if the Cold War persisted. Under the discriminatory regulations of the Doctor's Draft, physicians were drafted until they surpassed the age of 52 years. So in my third year at Michigan, I completed my premedical requirements, and with other courses, finished with 108 credit hours, only 12 hours short of graduating with a bachelor degree.

Courses

Professors of Comparative Anatomy, like those teaching Organic Chemistry, adhered to the notion that they had an obligation to screen out of the premedical program would-be doctors who lacked commitment. In Zoology, Dr. Stockard lectured rapidly and was ambidextrous. Holding a piece of colored chalk in each hand, he drew simultaneously on the blackboard the symmetrical sides of the body cavities of the dogfish shark and other animals we were to dissect. Trying to hold our colored pencils in one hand and our notebooks in the other, we frantic students raced to keep up. There were no note-taking services or cell phone cameras to help us. I enjoyed a course in Anthropology in which our prescient professor predicted the emergence of black pride and the rise of the Civil Rights Movement five years before they occurred.

Using an excellent volume of the complete works, annotated by our resident scholar G.B. Harrison, I explored, in an elective course, the comedies and tragedies of William Shakespeare. I read with pleasure each play four times to understand Elizabethan era idioms and humor. However, our effeminate professor, who referred to his students' roommates as she, thought little of my essay test answer about the role of Laertes in *Hamlet*. This led me to think less of the subjectivity involved in what my father called the "conversational subjects." Science was solid, understandable, objective, and satisfying, not influenced by the mood or whims of the observer. I have retained my well-worn copy of Harrison's textbook, referring to it before attending plays at the excellent Summer Shakespeare Festival at Winona State University.

DIVERSIONS

Sometimes on my way to South Quad after class, I strolled through the courtyard of The University of Michigan Law School Campus, transported to another world surrounded by buildings of gothic architecture, with gargoyles and stained glass windows, built to resemble those at Oxford University. I thought of my father working as student labor during the summer of 1920 with a crew to clear old houses from the site prior to the construction of these stone buildings. This was where my Uncle George graduated with honors and later served as District Attorney for Washtenaw County (Ann Arbor), and still later, represented his constituents in the US Congress for 14 years.

Members of the Biology Club, most of us were premedical students, met each month for a varied program. Especially memorable was the examination of bacteriophage through the new medium of electron microscopy. We learned how the phage virus injected its DNA into a cell commanding it to produce viral DNA, but I don't recall thinking about the next step; i.e., how it could be used to transmit other genomes to produce mammalian proteins. The field of genetic engineering was 30 years in the future. In another impressive session, we observed addicts lined up with arms extended for their daily intravenous injection of morphine, their daily "fix." These research subjects, a colony of rhesus monkeys in the Department of Pharmacology, were contributing to investigations designed to discover less addictive analgesics for patients with cancer and other painful illnesses. A professor of pharmacology present at our meeting told me that he had attended The University of Chicago Medical School. He said it was a great school, but the third year clinical clerkship was a bear! It was.

TUMOR RESEARCH PROJECT

In 1954-1955, I worked several hours a week as a part-time laboratory assistant for Walter J. Nungester, MD, PhD, Chairman, Department of Bacteriology. In his Tumor Research Project I helped his chief laboratory technician grow Ehrlich Ascites Tumor Cells in the peritoneal cavities of mice. We harvested the cells, processed them and injected them into rabbits to make antisera. Later, we obtained plasma from the rabbits and titered their antisera. Then we injected the antisera into mice to measure the protection it conferred against a challenge dose of the tumor cells. It was only years later, when I was performing cancer research in my own laboratory, that I realized the significance of Dr. Nungester's pioneering work on the immunotherapy of cancer.

One afternoon, Dr. Nungester walked into his laboratory to interrupt our work. With a smile, he asked us to take a break and have coffee and cookies with an official from the National Cancer Institute (NCI) who was in Ann Arbor coordinating a site visit review team for Michigan's research grant application. Why would he invite me to meet such a distinguished guest, I wondered? Entering the conference room, I saw the faculty investigators sitting on one side of a long table and the reviewers on the other. At the far end stood the tall coordinator of the visit, who laughed and said, "Hi, Dick. Have a cookie." The distinguished visitor turned out to be my Uncle Ralph who worked with Dr. Endicott of the NCI to coordinate extramural research funding. Michigan's favorable review won them the grant, not because I had anything to do with it.

Chapter XXIII

Transition and Decision 1955

APPLICATION TO MEDICAL SCHOOL

By the time I was in my junior year at Michigan, I had pestered my parents' friends with questions like, "Why did you decide to become a doctor?" In response, Dr. Paul Barker, Chairman of Medicine said, "I saw medicine as a way I could be of service to people." Other friends said that diagnosis of illness was like detective work, and that research in medicine to improve diagnosis and therapy was exciting, complementing the art of caring for fellow human beings. They said it was a "calling" that should not be undertaken unless one wanted to work hard and enjoyed people. None of the doctors I interviewed said that income had influenced their decisions.

Reflecting on my course work, it occurred to me I most enjoyed the rigor of chemistry, biology, physics, and psychology. I shared my mother's interest in people and the enjoyment she derived from helping them. All of this soul-searching—unnecessary for four of my high school classmates who already had made the decision to become doctors—was to be certain that a decision to go into medicine was mine and not one made just to please my father. In a meeting with Michigan's Dean of Students to discuss my plans, he told me of a student who had brought his physician father to the dean's office to announce that he decided not to apply to medical school.

The student's father was furious, leading the dean to realize that the student had sought his presence as a neutral witness to defend him from his father's wrath. My dad would never have behaved that way. He told me he would back me, whatever I decided to do.

Father had urged one of his former medical residents, an outstanding physician, to enter academic medicine. But Dr. Christian Schrock had returned from the army to set up a private practice in downtown Iowa City, disappointing my dad who thought Chris was giving up teaching and research for income. Hoping to secure another point of view regarding my dilemma, I sought Chris's opinion about the wisdom of applying to medical school. He dismissed the question with, "Of course, you should become a doctor! Whether you go into private practice or academic medicine after your training is the real question."

Realizing that physicians were always needed and served in a respected profession which cared for patients with skills based on science, I made my decision after my visit with Chris and applied to three medical schools: The Universities of Iowa, Michigan, and Chicago. Father had a sentimental attachment to Michigan, but he thought highly of the distinguished full-time faculty at The University of Chicago whom he had met in the Central Society for Clinical Research. Discovering that 1000 applicants from all over the country applied for the 72 places in Chicago's freshman class left me little hope of admission, but to my great pleasure and surprise, Dean Ceithaml's letter admitting me to Chicago was the first I received. Without waiting for the others to reply, I jumped at the chance and accepted by return mail.

SPRING 1955

During the spring of 1955, my last in Ann Arbor, the world of medicine focused upon two important events. Jerry Conn, MD, a Michigan faculty member and friend of my father's, was recognized for his discovery of primary aldosteronism, a surgically treatable form of hypertension, which some called Conn's disease. Later that spring, Dr. Tommy Francis of Michigan's School of Public Health announced the analysis of the successful clinical trials of the Salk vaccine to prevent poliomyelitis, bringing reporters with television cameras to broadcast the news from the front steps of the Michigan Union. Salk and later Sabin's vaccines eliminated a viral scourge that had killed and maimed thousands of children and young adults in the United States.

A less momentous event occurred on 14MAY1955, when seated at a round table at the Pretzel Bell Saloon, the bell was rung, and I was presented with a free pitcher of beer for my friends to toast attaining my majority. After my 21st birthday party, I walked back to South Quad under my own steam, unlike an acquaintance whose friends, after he consumed too many more pitchers, carried him back on a stretcher procured from Student Health.

Another event, unheralded but significant, occurred when Warren, our next door neighbor in Scott House, agreed to teach Gerry, his roommate, how to drive. Both were graduate students in Library Science, but their academic interests and room were all that they shared in common. Warren stemmed from Dutch heritage in Grand Rapids, Michigan. He was of medium height, dark complexion, and muscular with a generous paunch from a love of food and a history of hypothyroidism. He greeted issues, upsetting to most people, with a smile, calm slow speech, and unruffled demeanor. In marked contrast, Gerry was of Irish extraction, with bright red hair, freckles on a fair complexion, slightly taller than Warren, and thin as a rail. His movements were quick and his speech rapid, characteristic of New York City, whence he had come. At home, Gerry patronized the bus and subway, and now in his mid-twenties, admitted that he had ridden in an automobile only once in his life. Fascinated by the freedom from schedules an automobile provided in the Midwest, he implored Warren to teach him how to drive.

So every Sunday afternoon that spring, to hone Gerry's driving skills, Warren drove his 1937 Ford to the rural roads outside of Ann Arbor. When they reached a secluded county road with no traffic, Warren stopped his car and shifted to the passenger seat. Firmly, he grasped the emergency brake handle that arose from the hump in the center of the floor while Gerry, in the driver's seat clamped his hands on the steering wheel with a white-knuckle grip. Like his speech, Gerry's movements were a rapid staccato. Acceleration and braking were jerky, and his tendency to over- or under-correct steering turns would have landed them in the ditch had not Warren shouted, grabbed the wheel, and pulled the emergency brake. Returning to South Quad after practice, Gerry's grin and flushed face displayed a high state of exhilaration while with trembling hands, Warren rubbed his scalp with a look of sheer exhaustion. Somehow Warren survived the weekly ordeal. Gerry bought a used car, and without terrifying the patrolman, passed his driving test to obtain his license.

A Ride Home

Father's Sunday Letter of 22MAY1955 reported that he would be unable to drive me home from Ann Arbor, because he was committed to give two lectures and sophomores' oral examinations in his course on physical diagnosis in medical school at Iowa. I was glad to avoid that situation in the future by going to Chicago, not because he wasn't a good teacher, but as you might imagine, as the son of their professor, relations with my friends in the same class would be strained.

John Peckham, a friend from Scott House during our freshman year, kindly offered to give me a ride to Iowa after classes ended. John, had been recruited by Michigan from Sioux City, Iowa, to play football. His lineman's stature was topped by a shock of unruly red hair over a square face with red cheeks and freckles. His open friendly demeanor, typical of an Iowan, never betrayed his exalted status as a Wolverine football player. He wasn't the type of person easily rattled by difficulties.

Loading my suitcases in the dusty trunk of John's 1940 Chevrolet the afternoon of departure, I began to have second thoughts about riding with him. Dents and rusting of the lower parts of doors and running boards were not as unsettling as internal anomalies. After we got underway, I noticed the needle on the speedometer failed to budge from "zero." John said, "Don't worry. I will keep up with the traffic flow." Then I noticed the gasoline gauge registered "empty," but John assured me that he had just filled the tank. When he removed his foot from the accelerator to brake at a stoplight, I saw that the flat foot pedal, which should have covered the accelerator rod emerging from the floorboard, was missing.

We headed west on US 12 from Ann Arbor at about 5:00 PM, ignoring insignificant rattles and other defects without further incident. Later that night, we stopped at a highway café on US 6 west of Chicago to stretch our legs, get a sandwich and coffee, and fill the tank with gasoline. We spelled each other, driving through a moonlit night, to watch the sun rise in the rearview mirror. At dawn, we crossed the Mississippi River at Davenport to view Iowa's beautiful rolling hills, garnished in the green of emerging corn and soybeans, conveying a sense of openness, freedom and serenity after leaving the traffic of the bustling populous suburbs of Metropolitan Chicago.

Finally, we arrived in Iowa City at my parent's new home, their dream house, designed by my father with his architect-builder Wayne Paulson. It was a thrill to see it finished and occupied. We offered John a place to nap, but he declined and departed for the last 316-mile drive to Sioux City at the other side of the state.

Fortunately, before starting medical school at The University of Chicago in the month of September 1955, I found a job with Horrabin Construction Company, paving streets in Iowa City. For the first time in my 20 years in Iowa City, I lived in a house built by someone other than Howard Moffitt.

SELECTIVE SERVICE

In a file containing copies of my Captain's Commission, orders and discharge papers from the US Army, I recently found a copy of DD Form 398, Statement of Personal History. I had filled out this form when I was a Resident in Internal Medicine at The University of Chicago, anticipating an Armed Forces Physical Examination. Information therein has helped me recall, for the preceding narrative, residences, education, dates of employment and memberships in various organizations. I attested on the form that my membership in the National High School Honor Society, Phi Eta Sigma College Freshman Honor Society, Student Medical Association, and Alpha Omega Alpha National Medical Honor Society were neither Communist front organizations, nor had I ever been a Fascist or member of the Communist Party or a member of any group that advocated violent overthrow of the US Government. The Cold War would not end for another 30 years.

Before a dozen of us stripped for our physical examination at 7:00 AM on 16AUG1960 at the Selective Service Unit at 615 W. Van Buren Street in downtown Chicago, an Army Sergeant directed us to complete yet another detailed form. Helpfully guiding us through the items, anticipating questions, he said, "There are five boxes for item # 11 where you list your brothers and sisters. Start listing with the eldest. If you have more than 5, forget the rest of them. Do the same with item #12, telling you to list your children. If you have more than 5, forget 'em."

Next we proceeded through various stations where corpsmen measured blood pressure, pulse, temperature, obtained blood samples, and accepted urine samples. Then we lined up in front of one of the two physicians performing physical examinations, a black doctor in civilian clothes, who told us that he was going to examine us for inguinal hernias. As I was the only physician subject in the group, the examining doctor did me the honor—a fellow brother in the healing art—of examining me first.

Elwood, my classmate in medical school and a veteran, had told me that the Selective Service rarely rejected a doctor from serving in Army, saying, "If you are healthy enough to practice medicine as a civilian, you are healthy enough to practice in the Army." So, as we signed out at his desk, I asked the other physician in a Captain's uniform working there, "Have you ever classified a doctor 4F, unfit to serve in the Army?" He said, "Yes, one. The doctor had high blood pressure, out-of-control diabetes and an actively bleeding duodenal ulcer." Then, looking at my papers, he went on to say, "You are from the thinking man's hospital. I'm from the doing man's hospital, Cook County. Do you want a job here doing physical examinations?" Supplementing my salary of $225 per month made me hesitate before I declined to augment my 70 to 90-hour workweek—I wasn't just thinking all that time—with less leisure (sleep) and a commute from the South Side of Chicago.

Chapter XXIV
Friends of Moffitt Houses

An article in the 11MAY2011 *Gazette* announced an upcoming seminar by Jeff Schabilion: "Iowa City's Stone Buildings and Mr. Moffitt," sponsored by Friends of Historic Preservation (FHP) in recognition of National Preservation Month and Irving Weber Days. Scheduled for 2:30 PM, Saturday 14MAY2011, the seminar would serve as an introduction to Sunday's "Parade of Homes." The paper listed the addresses of the Moffitt houses on the tour, including one in which I had resided from 1946 to 1955 at 1203 Friendly Avenue. I had to overcome the realization that I had lived in an "historic home" only five years after it was built.

THE LECTURE

Leaning against the wind, driving a cold rain in our faces, we made our way on Linn Street to the Iowa City Library, early on Saturday to get a seat for the lecture. Karen and I could not imagine that an audience of more than a dozen people would show up for the talk. We got that wrong! A crowd of over 250 enthusiastic but damp "historians" filled all of the chairs in Meeting Room A, stood two deep in the back and overflowed into the hallway. Without even standing-room space, two of our friends who had arrived on time to hear their friend Jeff speak, gave it up and went home.

Jeff Schabilion described and showed examples of Iowa City's stone buildings from three eras. He illustrated with slides, The Settlement Period of the 1840's with photos of The Old Capitol, designed by John Rague and completed in 1842, built to serve as the capitol of Iowa Territory and later in 1846, the new State of Iowa. Jeff pointed out two different colored limestone blocks on the north face of the building. Some had been quarried near the University President's Home on Church Street, but the better quality white limestone had come from a quarry near North Liberty, he said.

As examples of The Beaux-Arts Classical Period of the 1890's to early 1900's, Jeff showed pictures of the buildings on the University Pentacrest: Schaefer, MacBride, MacLean, and Jessup halls. They were faced with Bedford Limestone and adorned with sculptures and Doric Columns. The old Biology Building (built for the medical school), the old Post Office and the old Carnegie Library, like the university buildings, represented institutional construction, too expensive for residential purchase.

Moffitt houses represented The Period of the Great Depression, the 1930's to the 1940's. These quaint houses of wood-frame construction were faced with rubble limestone pieces or stone foundation blocks of various sizes and shapes salvaged from nearby quarries. Our lecturer had an affinity for Moffitt houses. He lived in a Tudor-style Moffitt house on Rundell Street, several doors down the street from son Bill's friends, the Millers. Visiting the Miller's home, another Moffitt house, I was struck by the fact that the floor plan was nearly identical to the Moffitt house at 1218 Yewell Street, in which I had lived as a kid from 1935 to 1946.

CLOSE ENCOUNTERS AT THE HOUSE OF MOFFITT
A crisp breeze, warmed by generous sunlight, welcome after the cold blustery day before, greeted Karen and me as I drove to southeast Iowa City

for the Parade of Homes, Sunday 15MAY2011. Karen listened patiently while I pointed out where a vacant lot on Pickard Street once served as a childhood baseball/football field, but now was occupied by a house, built after Moffitt left town.

We walked south down the hill to the first house on the tour, a route I had taken many times in the past. In 1939, a second cousin of mine and his wife, Bob and Dotty, rented the house at 1215 Pickard Street when they arrived in Iowa City from Michigan for Bob to begin his internship at University Hospitals. Dotty raised their children there while Bob served as a Navy Medical Officer in the South Pacific during WWII. After Bob returned from the war, they moved to a house on Park Road, and he later became Professor and Head of Dermatology in the College of Medicine.

Seated at a card table by the sidewalk near the front door of the home at 1215 Pickard were three Friends of Historic Preservation wearing nametags, ready to accept our fees and to provide us with information. We recognized two of them: John Chadima of MidwestOne Bank and Attorney Jim Hayes. Several years earlier, Jim Hayes had graciously given us a tour of his home at 1142 Court Street, Grant Wood's former home, which Jim had beautifully restored, and would leave, with other properties, to the University as a residence for visiting artists.

"Tom Baldridge" on the nametag of the third Friend triggered a memory, leading me to ask this distinguished gentleman, wearing driving cap, tie, vest, and sport coat, "Was your father Dr. Baldridge?" "Yes, but I don't remember him. I grew up in Iowa City and spent my life in the Foreign Service returning here upon retirement," he said as best as I can recall his words. His father, Clarence W. Baldridge, MD, a senior colleague and friend of my father in the Department of Internal Medicine, was killed in an automobile crash in November 1934 while traveling to Fort Madison,

Iowa, to present a talk to physicians in the Lee County Medical Society. Later, reflecting that my mother had taken me with her to visit her friend and his widow, Mrs. Ada Baldridge and her children, I realized that I had played with this gentleman when we were kids.

The house at 1215 Pickard Street was typical of Moffitt's houses, limestone facing, large chimney on a small cottage-like abode with an attached single-car garage, converted by a subsequent owner to a family room. Yet it was charming and unique in that none of the other houses resembled each other on the blocks of Pickard Street and Friendly Avenue, a neighborhood referred to in the past as "Moffitt Hollow." I had visited this house many times as a child, but I had not remembered how narrow the stairway was to the bedrooms on the second floor. So, adults touring these cozy homes said, "Excuse me. No, that's OK, you go first," as they negotiated the narrow steps and filed into bedrooms large enough to hold a bed, a dresser, and a small chair, but only 3 or 4 visitors at one time. Close encounters, indeed.

1217 Pickard Street

Current owners of the homes at 1217 Pickard and 1111 Friendly expressed interest in my recollections of previous residents in their Moffitt houses, which I had visited many times as a teenager. Of course, these lovely brick houses seemed smaller than I remembered, but they were charming, evincing the current residents' skills at decorating and maintenance of their living spaces. At 1217 Pickard, there was a sunken living room with a large stone fire place at one end. Although I cannot remember their names, the persons who lived there were a warm friendly couple. I remember that the husband wore his white uniform home from University Hospitals where he was an instructor in Urology.

Jean and her children, Joan and Duncan, moved to Iowa City from Philadelphia for Jean to accept a teaching position at the University. They lived at 1111 Friendly Avenue in the 1940s while Jean's husband was serving overseas as a naval officer during WWII, a separation which ended permanently in divorce. When Joan, a stunningly beautiful girl, was in high school, her family lived next door at 1217 Friendly Avenue for too short a time. We had but one date. Jean moved to Mount Vernon, Iowa, to become Dean of Students at Cornell College leaving my father her recipe for Philadelphia Fish House Punch. It was a deceptively benign-tasting delicious, but powerful, libation causing one over-indulgent guest, walking home from a Sunday afternoon neighborhood party at my parent's house, to fall into a snow drift. Thank goodness, she wasn't driving!

Bob and Catherine, and their children followed Jean's family as renters of Moffitt's brick house at 1111 Friendly Avenue. Catherine, a beautiful woman in her 30s, wore short shorts while doing yard work, displaying lovely tanned legs, arousing my appreciation as an adolescent beginning to notice things like that. Bob was head of the Iowa City Chamber of Commerce, and later when I was a student at Michigan, he held the same post in Ann Arbor.

With their children, Ed and Dordana were the next occupants of the house at 1111 Friendly Avenue, living there for several years after my folks moved from the neighborhood in 1955. Dordana was a nutritionist and Ed was Professor of Surgery. He was a really nice guy, an outstanding surgeon, a nationally recognized pioneer in the field of bariatric surgery, introducing gastric bypass and stapling in the treatment of morbid obesity.

Why I didn't drag Karen to my old home at 1203 Friendly Avenue immediately upon laying eyes on it instead of following the sequence of the tour, I'm not sure, because I was anxious to see it and be inside the house again after 56 years. Perhaps it was the delayed gratification that I had experienced so frequently in my lifetime, saving the best for last. Walking around my old neighborhood brought back pleasant thoughts of living there while in high school and college from age 12 to 21 years, an impressionable time when everything seemed new and opportunities endless.

1203 FRIENDLY AVENUE

From the front porch of the house at 1111 Friendly, I gazed across the lawn at my former home at 1203 Friendly Avenue, impressed at how the lawn I had dutifully mowed, had diminished in area. I had watched Jesse Baker and his crew, build this house in 1941, but I do not know to whom Howard Moffitt rented it during WWII. My folks bought the house from Moffitt in 1946 and sold it in 1955 to a faculty member in Otolaryngology and his wife, a Dr. Tondorf. The couple was from Germany, and because he didn't want to mow the large lawn, my nemesis, or because of his "old country" culture, he erected a low stone garden wall around the house, enclosing low maintenance ground cover and trees. Since their occupancy, subsequent owners tastefully landscaped the yard, planting hostas, shrubs and more trees, reducing the size of the lawn, which required mowing, to practically nothing. What a great idea!

For the Parade of Homes this Sunday, the new owners of my former home had graciously opened their doors for the crowd on the tour. As Karen and I stepped through the front door of 1203 Friendly Avenue into the living room, a flood of images poured into my consciousness. There on the empty south wall was where my mother's old upright piano sat, entertainment for doctors and their wives, laughing and singing as Mother played popular songs from sheet music of the swing era during parties for these hard-working young people. A recovered couch on the east wall faced a stone fireplace on the west wall. Between them on the north was the end of the rounded living room, where windows, flanking a centrally placed bookcase, provided light for my father to read while he smoked his pipe in his big chair.

Perhaps it was her black hair and flashing dark eyes of our lovely hostess that triggered a memory of Barbara Whitby, a beautiful young nurse, seated at a card table in our living room many years ago. She was soon to be married to John Kennedy, a Foreign Service Officer in North Carolina. Despite tour-takers filing in and out of her home, our hostess listened patiently as I recalled entering my home (theirs now) at age 12 years to observe a gold-headed cane leaning against the front door jam. I was embarrassed to find myself the cause of hushed conversation among the dinner guests seated at white table cloth covered card tables in our living room. My mother kindly ushered me to the table of the guests of honor, introducing me to Sir Lionel and Lady Whitby and their lovely daughter, Barbara. Shy by nature, I mumbled greetings, but Sir Lionel put me at ease by asking, "Do you have an electric train?" I said, "Yes." Then he asked, "Is it a Lionel?" evoking a laugh from everyone.

Sir Lionel and Lady Ethel were both physicians for whom my mother had sent Care Packages containing food and toiletries to their home in London during the blitz, the Nazi bombings of WWII. Sir Lionel was an Internist-Hematologist whose patients included Prime Minister Winston Churchill and King George VI. Dr. Whitby and my father had corresponded regarding transfusion procedures in the US Army Blood Program in Europe, headed by Dad's former laboratory research assistant, Bob Hardin. In addition to visiting their soon-to-be son-in-law in North Carolina, the Whitbys had come to Iowa City to see my folks and Bob and Velma Hardin before returning to England when Sir Lionel would become Master of Cambridge University.

Bob Hardin had worked with Sir Lionel Whitby, coordinating Allied efforts to implement the transfusion of whole blood for the treatment of battlefield casualties, more effective than plasma infusion in the treatment of hemorrhagic shock. I treasure a book, inherited from my father: Whitby, Sir Lionel E.H. and Britton, C.J.C.: *Disorders of the Blood, Diagnosis: Pathology: Treatment: Technique*; J.&A. Churchill LTD, London, pp. 759, 1950. It is inscribed: "Elmer DeGowin/with kindest regards from/ Lionel Whitby."

After Sir Lionel died in 1951, Lady Ethel moved to an apartment in Hampton Court Palace, reserved by Queen Elizabeth II for those persons in "grace and favor," but she made a point of visiting my mother in Iowa City as late as 1970, during her trips to North Carolina to see her daughter and to Canada to see her son. Mother and she remained friends and correspondents until she died.

Our hostess, after patiently listening to my recitation, reluctantly agreed to let me see my old room up a steep narrow stairway, roped off to prevent Parade participants from venturing upstairs. As you would expect, the bedrooms and second bathroom upstairs were smaller than I had remembered them. The two small windows in my bedroom faced north, straddling the conical roof over the living room. There was room for a single bed, a desk and an old arm chair that provided comfort for reading and for my dog, Chum II, to sleep on its lumpy cushion. A south-facing window overlooking a vegetable garden in the backyard lighted my parents' "master bedroom," really too small to be called such.

The new owners slept downstairs in the larger bedroom across from the main bathroom. My father had used that room for his study, his desk under a north-facing window looking out at our front yard and up Pickard

Street. I remember seeing the blue glow of his fluorescent desk lamp in that window, walking home from the bus stop after going to a movie in the evening. I realized later that he was writing most of the chapters and editing the definitive text on blood transfusion, DeGowin, E.L., Hardin, R.C., Alsever, J.B.: *Blood Transfusion*, W.B. Saunders Co., Phildelphia & London, pp.587, 1949.

The Legacy of Howard Moffitt

In recounting this story of the 20 years Howard Moffitt built houses in Iowa City, telling what happened to my neighbors who lived in his houses, and relating the stories of my friends and myself during and after the 20 years I lived in a Moffitt house, it has occurred to me what remarkable opportunities we had living and working in Midwest America, "the flyover zone" as the east and west coasters refer to it.

Jeff Schabilion and the Friends of Historic Preservation deserve credit for publicizing the work and houses of Howard Moffitt for the 2011 National Historic Preservation Month and Irving Weber Days, especially since Iowa City's Historian, Irving Weber, failed to treat the subject in his *Iowa City Press-Citizen* columns relating the history of our community. At least I was unable to find an article about Moffitt houses in my eight volumes of reprints of his newspaper columns when I sought information about them. Fortunately, those writers who contributed the articles in the Winter 1992 issue of the *Palimpsest* 73: 147-160, 1992, provided us with a wealth of information, revealing the background and description of his houses and the entrepreneurial spirit of Howard Moffitt.

Affordable housing, defined by public officials, should cost less than 30% of a family's income. If one relates my family's annual income in 1946 of

$3,600 to rent for our Moffitt house at $50 per month or $600 a year, Howard Moffitt provided us with a home for 16.7% of my father's salary. Now there is a shortage of affordable housing in Iowa City, because developers find the cost of land too dear and building codes, red tape and other municipal and federal regulations insurmountable. According to a front page, below—the—fold article, Kiran Sood reported in *The Gazette* on 20APR2014 under the headline: "Affordable housing still hard to come by," that, "…there are only 11 affordable units per 100 extremely low-income households in Johnson County…" Without federal subsidies, taxpayer money, and charitable support, Howard Moffitt prevailed for 20 years, solving a problem that seems to defy solution now, only to be put out of business by federal rent controls.

It is a tribute to Howard Moffitt and his work that his small rental homes, built as affordable housing during the Great Depression for young university faculty members and other members of our community, are fully occupied 80 to 90 years later by the proud owners of their warm and cozy homes. Howard Moffitt's homes stand as testimony to his contributions to our city, yet a search in the Iowa City telephone directory of the listings of streets, avenues, courts, and roads failed to reveal any named Moffitt, nor could I find a building, school, park, or green space named for him, like those named for other worthy citizens. As a former occupant of Moffitt houses, I hope that efforts by the Friends of Historic Preservation will find an additional way to recognize Howard Moffitt's contributions to Iowa City with some suitable commemoration.

ACKNOWLEDGEMENTS

I thank William Nowysz—with his perspective of an experienced architect who has personally examined the building materials that Moffitt used—for providing valuable information about the quality of the materials and of the workmanship in the construction of Moffitt houses. I am grateful to Jeff Schabilion, who enjoys living in his Moffitt house, for his efforts in acquainting us with the houses, sharing his thoughts about them, and encouraging me to write about them.

We are indebted to the authors of the articles about Moffitt houses in the Winter 1992 issue of the *Palimpsest* for their contributions to our understanding of Moffitt's life and the setting in which he built affordable housing in Iowa City: Phil Miller, Jan Nash, Jeff Schabilion, and Linda Brown-Link.

The Iowa Summer Writing Festival course on Memoirs, taught by Jim McKean, Professor of English at Mount Mercy University, was a great experience, helping me to transition from technical writing to a narrative form. My friend, Ben Humphrey came from his home in Colorado to take Jim's course. Very helpful for me, were lectures by Brooks Landon, Professor of English at The University of Iowa, in his The Great Courses offering: *Building Great Sentences, Exploring the Writer's Craft.*

Vernetta Moe kindly read portions of the typescript and gave good suggestions. My University of Chicago Medical School classmate, a retired pediatric oncologist, now a writer and poet, Ben Humphrey, helped me stay with this effort. Nicholas Johnson, a friend since preschool, generously gave his time and his cogent advice for my project. I am grateful to him for sharing his perspective of growing up in Iowa City in writing the Foreword to this book.

A true lexophile (one who loves words), Steve Semken patiently taught me that you spell it Foreword (for a book), not Forward (for a cavalry charge). I greatly benefitted from his encouragement, editorial, and publishing skills, bringing this narrative to fruition through his Ice Cube Press.

I apologize if lapses of memory have omitted facts and the valuable contributions of other persons not mentioned in the book. If I have failed to catch errors or other inaccuracies, please forgive me, for despite my bride's sarcastic admonition, "Well, Mr. Perfect!" I am not perfect. Without hesitation, and with patience, my wife Karen, and son Bill, have encouraged me in this endeavor as they have for other undertakings in the past.

About the Author

Richard L. DeGowin, MD, FACP, Professor Emeritus, Department of Internal Medicine, Division of Hematology, The University of Iowa, lives in Iowa City with his wife, Karen. He graduated from University of Iowa High School and attended The University of Michigan to complete his premedical studies. He received his MD and residency training at The University of Chicago. After discharge from two years' active duty in the US Army Medical Corps, he accepted a position as Assistant Professor of Medicine and Project Supervisor, Argonne Cancer Research Hospital of The University of Chicago. He returned to Iowa City as Associate Professor of Medicine, Section of Hematology with a joint appointment in the Radiation Research Laboratory and as Attending Physician at The University of Iowa Hospitals and Clinics and at The Veterans Administration Hospital. He was the Founding Director of The University of Iowa Cancer Center. He served as coauthor with his father for the first four editions of *DeGowin's Diagnostic Examination*, and for the five subsequent editions after his father died in 1980. Now in its tenth edition, it has been in print for 50 years, with translations into German, French, Italian, Spanish, Greek, Portuguese, and Chinese. He received the Laureate Award from the Iowa Chapter of the American College of Physicians, and while attending his 50th Year Medical School Reunion, he received The Distinguished Service Award of The University of Chicago.

The Ice Cube Press began publishing in 1993 to focus on how to live with the natural world and to better understand how people can best live together in the communities they share and inhabit. Using the literary arts to explore life and experiences in the heartland of the United States we have been recognized by a number of well-known writers including: Gary Snyder, Gene Logsdon, Wes Jackson, Patricia Hampl, Greg Brown, Jim Harrison, Annie Dillard, Ken Burns, Roz Chast, Jane Hamilton, Daniel Menaker, Kathleen Norris, Janisse Ray, Craig Lesley, Alison Deming, Harriet Lerner, Richard Rhodes, Michael Pollan, and Barry Lopez. We've published a number of well-known authors including: Mary Swander, Jim Heynen, Mary Pipher, Bill Holm, Connie Mutel, John T. Price, Carol Bly, Marvin Bell, Debra Marquart, Ted Kooser, Stephanie Mills, Bill McKibben, Elizabeth McCracken, Dean Bakopoulos, and Paul Gruchow. Check out Ice Cube Press books on our web site, join our facebook group, follow us on twitter, visit booksellers, museum shops, or any place you find good books and discover why we continue striving to, "hear the other side."

Ice Cube Press, LLC (est. 1993)
205 N. Front Street
North Liberty, Iowa 52317-9302
steve@icecubepress.com
twitter @icecubepress
www.icecubepress.com

to Laura Lee & Fenna Marie
two glorious history makers